British Legion 4773210
Harcourt Center
11 Rd

BLOOD AND MONEY

Dave Copeland

BLOOD
AND
MONEY

The True Story of Ron Gonen:
Gangster Turned FBI Informant

Every effort has been made to contact the copyright holders of material reproduced in this text. In cases where these efforts have been unsuccessful, the copyright holders are asked to contact the publishers directly.

First Published by Barricade Books as *Blood and Volume* in 2007.
Published by Maverick House Publishers.
Maverick House, Main Street, Dunshaughlin, Co. Meath, Ireland.
Maverick House Asia, Level 41, United Centre, 323 Silom Road, Bangrak, Bangkok 10500, Thailand.

info@maverickhouse.com
http://www.maverickhouse.com

ISBN: 978-1-905379-44-6

5 4 3 2 1

Printed and bound in the UK
by Cox & Wyman Ltd, Reading, Berkshire

The paper used in this book comes from wood pulp of managed forests. For every tree felled, at least one tree is planted, thereby renewing natural resources.

A CIP catalogue record for this book is available from the British Library.

'Ron Gonen is a despicable person. Ron Gonen has a record of crime that extends almost to the time he reached maturity.... You don't have to like Ron Gonen. But you do have to listen to him.'

— Gary Cutler, Assistant US Attorney,
30 October 1991

For my parents.

CONTENTS

AUTHOR'S NOTE

THIS BOOK IS a work of non-fiction based on hundreds of hours of interviews and an extensive review of all available law enforcement and court documents regarding the members of the Israeli Mafia that operated in New York City in the 1980s.

No names have been changed, although there were cases in which certain names were spelled several different ways. In some cases the same person's name would be spelled as many as four different ways in a single document. For the sake of consistency, I have used the most common spelling of the name throughout the book. For people who have entered the Witness Protection Programme following the events depicted in this book, I have used their pre-programme names.

Much of the narrative of *Blood & Money* is based on Ron Gonen's point of view and, to a lesser extent, the perspective of his wife, Honey Tesman. However, these are not Ron Gonen's words, and in every possible instance, I have fact checked the information he provided and have supplemented it with information from third-party sources, interviews, and documents. If something Gonen or any other source told me could not be verified, it was not included.

Dialogue was either taken directly from court testimony, wiretaps, or other documents, or was reconstructed by interviewing all available participants of a conversation and arriving at as close to a consensus of what was as possible and taking into account the limits of human memory.

PREFACE

RON GONEN AND I met the way so many people meet these days: we met on Craigslist, the Web site where you can get a date, used furniture, a roommate or your very own ex-gangster.

In November 2004, I was desperately trying to come up with a topic for my master's thesis in creative non-fiction writing from Goucher College. I decided I would write about life inside the federal Witness Protection Programme, with one obvious obstacle in my way: As far as I knew, I didn't know anyone living in the programme.

I was working as a freelance writer and skimming the job ads on Craigslist when I came across one that seemed too perfect. It was written by Gonen's wife—Gonen doesn't like computers—and it calmly explained that she and her husband were living in the Witness Protection Programme and looking for a writer to tell their story.

I immediately responded and more than a month later, on Christmas Day 2004, Honey Tesman, Gonen's wife, finally e-mailed back. It was a short message, but she gave enough hints to let me know that they had been involved in organised crime. I immediately responded and manically checked my e-mail throughout the holiday. After a week without hearing from them, I assumed they had gone with a different writer.

In January 2005, I was living in Pittsburgh. It was Saturday, 22 January, and I was hanging out at my apartment, waiting for a snow storm to start and trap me in for the weekend. The phone rang and on the other end was a man with a thick accent. It was part Russian, part Israeli, and I could've sworn I even detected the faintest hint of New York in his voice. We talked for two hours, and Gonen gave me the rough overview of his life.

From the perspective of a journalist, his story was perfect: A jewel and art thief in Europe and the Middle East in the 1970s, Gonen had moved to New York in the 1980s and started dealing cocaine. He fell in with a group of Israeli criminals who were vicious killers, and, just a few days before he was to have been executed, Gonen was whisked into the Witness Protection Programme. The story was dripping with greed, sex, clever crimes, and colourful personalities. I quickly re-evaluated my story: It wasn't life in the Witness Protection Programme—complete with mundane jobs and minivans—that was interesting. The interesting story was what you did to get yourself there in the first place.

And Gonen did a lot, not least of which was help federal authorities bring down what the New York City tabloids and Israeli dailies called the 'Israeli Mafia.' We spoke for several hours each day for the next few weeks. The book you now hold is the product of hundreds of hours of research and interviews and is an accurate depiction of events as they happened.

Gonen understood from the outset that this was a work of journalism and my goal would be to depict the events of his life accurately, even if they did not portray him in a good light.

THE PURPOSE OF *Blood & Money* is twofold. First, I wanted to document the inner workings of an organised crime syndicate that got very little press while terrorising the outer boroughs of New York in the 1980s. Johnny Attias' Israeli Mafia took part in everything from contract murders to setting up an international drug trafficking network that brought heroin to the United States from Europe and Southeast Asia and moved cocaine from North America to the Middle East. Had they not been so brazen in their crimes and so bloodthirsty in their means of retribution, the Israeli Mafia could have filled the void created by the systematic decimation of the Italian Mafia by the RICO statutes. Additionally, the Israeli Mafia paved the way for the Russian Mob to gain control of the New York underworld after the fall of the Soviet Union in 1990.

But the most important thing I learned—and the element of the story best illustrated by weaving this book around the narrative that is Ron Gonen's life—is just how hard it is to be a career criminal. There is a certain self-centred confidence that every good criminal has, and Gonen—even after sixteen years in the Witness Protection Programme—maintains that swagger. At times I found his lack of remorse infuriating, but after a while, it made a certain sense: To commit crimes against others, whether it be looting their apartment of every last valuable or hooking them on a drug as deadly as cocaine, people have to believe that they are more important than whomever they come in contact with. It makes a certain sense, but it also strikes me as a tough way to go through life.

Beyond the attitude, however, are the day-to-day complexities of being a gangster. Gonen worked hard, and his wife, Honey Tesman, often told me if he had worked as hard at a straight profession as he had at being a felon, he could have been anything he wanted to be. He kept long hours, and, at least during the first few years he was in New York, he used the drugs he was selling to fuel his frantic pace. A typical day would take him to the far corners of New York City to pick up and drop off drugs and money. When most people mess up at their job, they get reprimanded or, at worst, fired. When Gonen messed up, he went to jail. And when he really messed up, he was nearly killed. He sacrificed time with his daughter and had strained relationships with his parents, his half-sister, and his wife. In the end he had almost nothing to show for three decades as a gangster. And based on what I learned about his accomplices, they all worked just as hard and in almost every case met fates similar to or worse than Gonen's.

The goal of this book is not to glorify Ron Gonen or the criminal life. But given the hundreds of true crime titles published and the dozens of movies produced each year, the world has a strong fascination with the gangster lifestyle. This is simply the story of one of those gangsters.

- *Dave Copeland, Boston, Massachusetts, August 2006.*

PROLOGUE

The Blood and the Money

Newark, New Jersey, 27 September 1989

JOHN GUSLAVAGE SHIFTED in the two office chairs serving as his makeshift bed. While the chairs were uncomfortable, what was really keeping him awake was the fact that he might have thrown his career away on the man behind the steel door he faced.

All day and, now, all night, Guslavage had been in this bunker of an office in a federal building in Newark, New Jersey.

Guslavage was an Elizabeth narcotics cop and part of a special task force made up of DEA officials, IRS accountants, immigration and naturalisation officers, and FBI agents. The task force was charged with finding drug dealers like Ron Gonen, who sat in the small, windowless holding cell behind the door.

Guslavage was still wearing the dark jeans and open-collar shirt he had been wearing when he arrested Gonen, and he was using his black leather jacket as a blanket. He was forty-five, tall and fit, and bore a striking resemblance to NBA coach Pat Riley—after studying his long face and combed-back hair for a few hours, Gonen told him as much. Guslavage didn't laugh at the joke, but quietly admitted to himself that there was something endearing about Gonen.

For more than three months, the agents had listened and watched as Gonen arranged high-priced cocaine deals on the telephone. For the past three days, they had staked out his Manhattan apartment, across the street from the Museum of Natural History. And finally, as Gonen emerged that morning from a corner store near the apartment carrying a carton of milk and a grapefruit, they arrested him.

At first Gonen had remained tight-lipped and remarkably calm for a man facing ten years to life in prison on each of the six counts of conspiracy to distribute cocaine that he faced. It was only late in the afternoon that Gonen had begun to understand how much trouble he was in. His wife arrived soon after, with several grams of cocaine in her system, an open bottle of wine in her backpack, and a high-priced criminal defence attorney at her side. Gonen had used his one phone call to tell Honey Tesman to find a good attorney and head over to New Jersey. After meeting with her husband, Tesman was escorted by their attorney into a long, tile-lined corridor.

'This is fucking entrapment!' she screamed at the agents who filtered in and out of the office. It was nearing 6pm when Gonen's lawyer met with his client in a conference room. 'You can plead not guilty, pay me more than a quarter of a million dollars in legal fees, and still wind up in prison,' the attorney said. 'Or you can take your chances, pay me $100,000, co-operate, and plead guilty.'

The office was an open, 2,000–square-foot space with tables and desks scattered throughout. Gonen and his attorney sat at a table on one side of the office empty of agents. Gonen did some calculations—even if he got off with fifteen years, his life was over. He had been battling cancer and knew if he jumped bail, he would not be able to get the treatments he needed. His wife was a cocaine addict and leaving her behind would surely mean that Tesman and their daughter, Mariel, would end up on the welfare line. Gonen waved for Guslavage, who was standing by his own desk across the room. 'I'm going to talk,' he said, 'but I need a few things from you.'

'What do you need?'

Gonen assured Guslavage that the following morning, when all the attorneys and investigators were back for another day of work, he would be able to give them information on a wide range of criminal activities that would make his six cocaine charges look like jaywalking. But if Gonen wasn't allowed to answer incoming pages or, even worse, if he were put in a general jail population where people would recognise him, he would not only be unable to help them build cases against some of New York's most notorious underworld figures, but his wife and daughter would be killed.

There was no reason for Guslavage to trust Gonen. He had already run Gonen's fingerprints through Interpol and gotten a preliminary report: Not only had Gonen masterminded a German prison break in 1978, but he was also a leading suspect in a London fraud ring that had stolen more than $4 million in merchandise between 1979 and 1981. He was tied to a series of unsolved art and jewellery thefts in Germany in the 1970s, and had been exiled from his native Israel.

'I don't know, Ron,' Guslavage said. 'Even if I did want to trust you, what am I supposed to do with you tonight? We have to take you to jail. There's no other place to keep you.'

'What about there?' Gonen said, pointing to the small holding cell in the corner of the expansive office.

The office was an office, not a jail and not a place where prisoners were kept overnight. The cell itself was actually a small, converted storage room that had been reinforced with a steel door. It was not meant for holding people for more than a couple of hours during their first round of questioning, before they were shipped off to jail for the night. It was 12 feet by 12 feet, with exposed concrete walls. It had no windows, no furniture, and a single, fluorescent light tube. A simple steel door was the room's only entrance. Suspects could be held there between booking and questioning, but federal building policy made it clear that under no circumstances were prisoners to be kept in the cell—in the unguarded building—after regular working hours. If something went wrong, if word got out that Guslavage had okayed the decision to keep a suspect there—and then allowed that suspect to place and receive calls to underworld associates—he would be back to walking a beat in Elizabeth.

'Wait,' Guslavage said. 'Let me see what I can do.'

John Cipriano, a jovial, Irish-looking DEA agent, headed the task force. Despite his good nature, he was even warier of allowing Gonen to spend the night in the building. Cipriano had white hair and blue eyes and a friendly demeanour, but he remained a by-the-book type of guy. He felt Gonen was a garden-variety cocaine dealer: relatively high up on the food chain, but not the kind of dealer who would be able to lead them to bigger busts. He didn't think Gonen had too much information to offer, but he also knew that good cops like Guslavage built good cases on hunches.

'You're staying here with him all night,' Cipriano said, adding that if something went wrong, Guslavage—not Cipriano—would be liable.

When the office was nearly empty, Guslavage carted a stack of bullet proof vests to the cell. These would serve as Gonen's mattress for the night. He brought him toilet paper, an ashtray, and a pack of Winstons. He also provided a plastic bucket that would serve as Gonen's toilet as well as a bag of potato chips and two cans of Coke that would be his dinner.

Throughout the course of the night, Gonen would tap on the door. When Guslavage opened the door, Gonen would show him the number displayed on his electronic pager and say, 'I need to answer that.'

Guslavage would write down the telephone number and start the recording equipment. Gonen would make a call, then explain to the person on the other end that he was doing business in Canada and would see him or her when he returned. He would then let Guslavage escort him back to the cell.

Sometimes Guslavage would hear the muffled sound of the beeper going off in the cell, but Gonen wouldn't tap on the door.

'Do you need to answer that, Ron?' Guslavage would yell.

'No,' Gonen would respond. 'It's just some junkie. They won't even remember that they called me in the morning.'

On one trip to make a phone call he allowed Gonen to stretch his legs outside of the cell.

'Tell me something, Ron. You're a career criminal. When we get in that room tomorrow, why should I believe a single word you say?'

Although his entire life had revolved around stings and scams, Gonen had never thought of himself as a career criminal. Guslavage's words hit him like a punch in the stomach. He took a long drag on his cigarette and collected his thoughts.

'My wife said if I had had parents like hers, parents who stressed education and going to college, I could have been anything I wanted,' Gonen said. 'I could have been a surgeon, I could have been a lawyer. I even could have had your job.'

Guslavage chuckled. Gonen was 41 and had a thick Russian accent, with the time he spent in Germany, Israel, and New York colouring his speech as well. But after listening to his recorded telephone conversations for hours, Guslavage had no trouble understanding what Gonen was saying.

'But I didn't, so I did what I did,' Gonen said. 'And now I hate it. In the past five years, I've beaten drug addiction and cancer and fathered a beautiful baby girl. For the past two years, I've been trying to get out of it, but when we talk tomorrow you'll see there were complications, threats to my life and my family's life.'

Gonen stood to let Guslavage lead him back to the cell. 'So you call me a career criminal,' Gonen said. 'But it doesn't mean I want to be one forever.'

As the first hints of dawn crept through the office windows, the pager's urgent beeping trailed off. But still, Guslavage could not sleep.

THE NEXT MORNING, Gonen called Honey Tesman from the phone on Guslavage's desk. As he pretended to shuffle through some paperwork, Guslavage could hear her yelling through the phone—loud enough for him to make out the words 'entrapment' and 'fight it.' Gonen, however, was firm. He told her not to come to the federal building in Newark that day. 'And if you see anyone, just act normal. Tell them I'm in Canada,' Gonen said.

Tesman said something that Guslavage could not hear. 'We still have more than a week to Yom Kippur,' Gonen said. 'I know it will look bad if I'm not there, but we just need to get through today.'

Gonen hung up. 'She thinks I should fight it,' he said. 'She thinks it's entrapment.'

'Is she a lawyer?' Guslavage said. Gonen laughed.

Gonen looked like a man who hadn't slept in 24 hours, but he still seemed calm. The designer jeans he had been arrested in were rumpled from a night in the cell, and he left his grey Nike running shoes unlaced. He had done his best to clean himself up when Guslavage had escorted him to the men's washroom.

Gonen's attorney arrived promptly at nine, and after conferring with his client for a few minutes in a conference room, Gonen signalled that they were ready to begin. As the investigators filed past Guslavage into the conference room, Cipriano stopped and pulled close to the Elizabeth police officer. 'This better be good,' he said just loud enough for Guslavage to hear.

Gonen's smile did not register in his eyes, which remained firm and dark. He was 6 feet 1 inch tall, the same height as Guslavage, and cast an imposing presence over the room. He had brown hair and was going bald. He was charming and likable, but he was also a criminal. When law enforcement agents had debriefed one of the informants who had helped them nab Gonen, the informant had told them that Gonen often bragged of individually breaking the fingers of a man who owed him money.

When everyone was in the room and Gonen was seated at the conference table, Cipriano casually leaned back and started his interrogation.

'So, Ron, what are we going to talk about today?' Cipriano said. 'What do you want?' Gonen said. 'I have a lot to tell you.'

'Like what?' Cipriano said.

'We could start with the $4 million gold robbery in Manhattan, followed by the $4 million insurance fraud,' Gonen said. 'Or maybe you want to hear about the drug smuggling ring I know about—cocaine from here to Europe and the Middle East and heroin from Amsterdam to here.'

Cipriano remained collected. Years of working as a cop had helped him perfect his poker face. 'I also know of at least six murders,' Gonen said. 'A contract murder for the Italians, two for revenge, and three that were just done in cold blood.'

Throughout the morning, Gonen talked. Investigators would leave and return—sometimes a few minutes, sometimes a few hours, later. They would give an affirmative nod in Cipriano's direction, indicating that Gonen's story had checked out with investigators working on those cases in different jurisdictions.

Cipriano finally had to stop the prisoner. 'For now, all we want to hear about is blood and money.'

'Blood and money?' Gonen asked.

'Murders and big cocaine deals,' replied Cipriano. 'Or blood and volume. Whatever you want to call it. If you tell us about the smaller stuff, we're required to investigate it, and, quite frankly, we just don't have the manpower to look into everything you seem to know about.'

Guslavage exhaled deeply. It looked as if his gamble on Ron Gonen was about to pay off.

IN ONE SENSE, the officers and prosecutors had built a solid case against a notorious drug dealer and a very bad man. Their facts and evidence lined up, and they were correct in assuming that Gonen would have little chance of winning his case if he went to trial. But in another sense, they failed.

In months of listening to Gonen and tailing him and his best friend, Ran Ephraim, through New York City, New Jersey, and Long Island, they had failed to pick up on the bigger picture. They failed to draw the connection between Gonen, Ephraim, and their Israeli friends and the string of grisly murders that tabloid reporters had already started to speculate were being conducted by a group they called the 'Israeli Mafia.'

The Israeli Mafia was short on numbers—at its peak, its core membership numbered fewer than 20 men—and it was not an organised crime syndicate like the Italian Mafia or the Russian Mob. There were no layers of tradition, no clear-cut hierarchies, and no codes of criminal conduct. It was a scary organisation to be affiliated with. The Italian mafia's *Omerta* code dictated that members could not kill one another without valid reasons. Israeli Mafia members were free to kill each other at will.

The gang, at least in the United States, was also short-lived; they filled a brief void between the decline of the Italian Mafia's influence in the mid-1980s and the rise of the Russian Mob, which followed the fall of the Soviet Union. Johnny Attias, the Israeli Mafia's de facto leader for almost all of its existence, arrived in New York City in 1984. By September 1990, all the gang's core members had either been arrested, entered the Witness Protection Programme, fled the country, or been murdered.

But the sheer number of crimes they committed, as well as Attias' unwillingness to play by accepted underworld rules, made them far more ferocious than their small size would suggest. Ran Ephraim was the mastermind of the biggest gold robbery in the history of Manhattan's Diamond District, and Attias helped him double his take by threatening jewellers who demanded reimbursement when the insurance cheques were cut. Without the DEA even realising it, Attias had become the tri-state area's biggest importer of heroin. And perhaps most frightening of all, he saw killing as one of the perks of his chosen profession.

The premise behind the gang's brash behaviour—an inaccurate premise, as it turned out—was that they could commit crimes at will and not fear long prison sentences. At the time Israel would not extradite an Israeli national to face trial for capital crimes committed in a foreign country, including the United States. Attias told the men working with him that if they were ever arrested he would bail them out and help them flee back to Israel. In the words of Eric Seidel, a former assistant district attorney in Brooklyn who helped Israeli officials prosecute two of the gang's members, 'They viewed America as their personal cookie jar. They thought they could steal as much as they wanted and get away with it.'

And to a large extent, they did, all while helping Attias carve out a deadly reputation. Attias stood up to the Italian Mafia and edged into the rackets of the fledgling Russian Mob. The Italians were so impressed with Attias that instead of killing him for infringing on their businesses, they outsourced contract killings to him.

What the Italians did not know when they hired Attias was that he was a clumsy killer. While staking out one target, he was arrested and charged with possession of a firearm. While shooting another, he hissed the name of his accomplice. But this ineptitude did not stop him from enjoying and even excelling at murder. He killed at least six men in New York, and at least one of the murders involved torturing the victim for 12 hours. Attias also told Gonen he had killed more people in Europe and the Middle East before arriving in New York.

And, eventually, Attias started hinting that he wanted to kill Ron Gonen.

It was nothing personal. Ron Gonen was one of Manhattan's better cocaine dealers in the 1980s. Gonen sold drugs retail to friends and people he met in nightclubs and wholesale to drug dealers throughout the world. He portrayed himself not as a dealer but as someone who always managed to find high-quality cocaine at a good price.

Even with his low-key persona, however, Gonen was among New York City's best-known cocaine dealers by the time the DEA caught up with him. When he started out, Gonen peddled drugs in nightclubs with the help of his wife, Honey Tesman. When other dealers were selling grams of cocaine cut with inert agents for $75, Gonen was selling pure cocaine for $45 a gram. Eventually his business grew, and he started dealing by the kilo. He became an international drug smuggler, purchasing kilos in New York for $15,000 or $16,000 and selling them in Europe and the Middle East for as much as $60,000. At his peak, Gonen was one step removed from a Colombian cocaine cartel and, in a good month, netted $100,000 for what amounted to a few hours of work each day.

Attias was smuggling drugs in the opposite direction. A kilo of heroin could be purchased in Amsterdam or Southeast Asia for $30,000, flown to New York, cut up, broken into packets for individual users, and sold in Brooklyn and Queens for as much as $300,000. But Attias had trouble breaking into the Manhattan market.

Unlike Gonen, Attias was not fluent in English and did not feel comfortable operating any place where it would not be appropriate to wear one of his $200 Adidas warm-up suits. Attias knew that Gonen was dealing with a higher class of clientele than the men he employed to sell drugs to junkies. He suspected if he could get Gonen to turn his cocaine customers onto heroin, he could double or even triple his take.

At first Attias put friendly pressure on Gonen through their mutual friend Ran Ephraim. When Gonen politely refused, Attias increased the pressure. Gonen had always considered himself an independent gangster, and he saw nothing but trouble coming if he got tied up with Attias. Ephraim dropped hints about the gang's lucrative stings, but Gonen fixated on the bodies piling up in the wake of the Israeli Mafia. Beyond that, Gonen claims that by the late 1980s he was trying to go straight.

He had enrolled in night school to get his realtor's license, and, with an infant daughter and a wife addicted to cocaine, Gonen was hoping to go clean. A cancer diagnosis helped Gonen stall Attias, but by 1989 Ran Ephraim was telling Gonen that Attias was increasingly frustrated with his refusals. Attias had even contemplated killing Gonen to make a point to other Israeli criminals in New York. You did not say 'no' to Johnny Attias.

GONEN GOT ARRESTED just in time to save his life— another few months out on the street, Ran Ephraim later told prosecutors, and someone in the Israeli Mafia would have killed him.

Gonen's plans to become a realtor had been derailed when he learned that New York State did not grant licenses to foreigners. He was facing ten years to life on each of the six counts of conspiracy to distribute cocaine he had been charged with, but, with a little luck and a lot of cooperation, Gonen could get a new start in the Witness Protection Programme.

Around the time New Jersey–based agents were moving in on Gonen, a Long Island contractor visited the US attorney's office on Long Island. The man had become sceptical when Raz Ben-Zvi, an Israeli jeweller who had been robbed twice in a six-year span, had paid for a $20,000 addition to his home—all in $10 bills.

At first investigators in New York and New Jersey worked independently and were oblivious to the fact that their two investigations were barely scraping the surface of a gang that had the potential to become one of the deadliest underworld organisations in New York City. But the probes soon dovetailed and, in a huge but grossly underreported law enforcement victory, the gang's New York operations were completely broken within a year.

On 27 September 1989, Gonen realised that beyond getting a new chance to start over as an anonymous man in an anonymous city, he had a chance to bring the gang down. If you have never heard of the Israeli Mafia before now, you have Ron Gonen's willingness to make a deal and co-operate to thank.

1

PORTRAIT OF A GANGSTER AS A YOUNG HOOD

THERE WERE THREE of them, and they met every few weeks in a dingy Los Angeles motel room. It was 1982. In a sense they were to cocaine dealing what other men their age were to the emerging computer industry—innovators, taking what had been a niche industry with expensive products and carving out a mass market. Both were risky business ventures, but both had the potential for huge payoffs. Ron Gonen was always the guest at these meetings. He was there to meet his old friend, Ran Ephraim, a fellow Israeli and, like Gonen, a lifelong criminal. Ran Ephraim had spent most of the previous year in Peru and Colombia, finding sources for pure cocaine. Once he had found the source—the third man, who went by the name of Mango—Ephraim had set up shop in Los Angeles. It was his motel room, and it was, by all accounts, a sad and lonely place.

Ephraim had found pure cocaine and a supplier willing to fly several kilos of the drug to Los Angeles each month. What he hadn't found were customers.

He had no talent for opening up markets. Ephraim was antisocial—he had served in the Israeli military and then had worked as a merchant marine before becoming a full-time criminal in the early 1970s. A big man at 6 feet 2 inches tall and 220 pounds, he wore his hair in a crew cut. In Israel, the other gangsters had called him Blondie, but now in America his hair was getting darker and turning grey. He had a hardened gaze and typically wore combat boots and cargo pants. His presence didn't exactly put potential cocaine customers at ease.

Enter Ron Gonen, his friend from the days in Israel when Ephraim used to fence the jewellery and collectibles Gonen had boosted from hotel rooms and parked cars. Gonen's problem was the opposite—he was trying to sell cocaine in Tel Aviv nightclubs, but his supply route meant a trip to Amsterdam every week to buy low-quality cocaine by the gram from street dealers. Gonen was charming and genuinely liked by most everyone he met—he had solid, good looks and an athletic build similar to Ephraim's. He was going bald, but he off set that one deficiency with a gregarious smile.

Before meeting Ephraim and Mango in Los Angeles for the first time, Gonen had been in America only once before. He spent ten days in New York City in December 1981 after fleeing Guatemala on an emergency visa as a civil war erupted in the country. During those ten days, Gonen became a fixture at the famed Chelsea Hotel, which billed itself as 'a rest stop for rare individuals'; it had been home to a host of writers, musicians, and artists of varying degrees of notoriety. Though Gonen had initially flown to Los Angeles to buy cocaine to sell in Tel Aviv, he soon found that by working a New York layover into his return trip he could double or even triple the amount of cocaine he was selling by unloading a chunk of it on his newfound friends at the Chelsea. By the middle of 1982, he had moved to New York permanently.

The Los Angeles meetings were tense, at least as long as Mango was around. Mango was jittery, a cocaine dealer who used too much of his product. As the buyer, Gonen was naturally at odds with Mango, but the tension increased because Gonen simply didn't like Mango. Ephraim was the broker; for every kilo Gonen bought, Mango would pay him a commission— usually between $500 and $1,000 per kilo. They would conduct their transactions with efficiency on the room's particle board table, then smoke cigarettes and talk—never acknowledging the tens of thousands of dollars in cash and cocaine they had between them. Everyone was carrying at least one gun. Mango was usually high, and Ephraim was naturally nervous. After one transaction Mango placed the tools of the just-completed deal into a briefcase: two kilos wrapped tightly in plastic, a jeweller's scale, a couple of razor blades, and a handful of sandwich bags.

'You look like shit,' Ephraim said to Mango.

'I can't sleep anymore,' Mango said.

Mango was paranoid from too much cocaine, too many cigarettes, and now, he confessed, a lack of sleep. Gonen asked if it was indeed the drug that had caused his dishevelled appearance.

'No, I'm trying to lay off this shit,' Mango said. 'Too many nightmares.'

He snapped his briefcase shut without taking his eyes off Gonen.

'Every night,' Mango said as he stood to leave, 'I have these dreams. I have these dreams where I kill my children.'

Gonen didn't flinch. He had been a gangster for more than a decade and he knew better than to appear shocked. He had served time in two different German prisons, and he had stared down criminals more ferocious than Mango. He knew that Mango was playing a head game, trying to see if Gonen was tough enough to be trusted with their newfound venture.

Gonen naturally despised Mango because Mango was a drug dealer, overlooking the fact that he himself was becoming a dealer of note in both New York and Tel Aviv.

RON GONEN DESPISED drug dealers because he had been classically trained as a criminal. He had been trained to view drug dealers as a lower class of criminals, the way an accomplished journalist might look down on a *National Enquirer* reporter.

Today, Gonen would have you believe he was predestined to be a gangster. Gonen was born Roman Gershman in 1948 in the Ukraine, the only son of working-class parents. He would change his name to the less-ethnic sounding Ron Gonen while living in Israel in the late 1960s. Gonen had an older half-sister, his mother's daughter by a previous husband who didn't return from the front after World War II.

His father, Jacob Gershman, was Polish and had fled the Nazi occupation in 1939. He had served in the Russian military during World War II and earned the nickname 'the Loyal Pollack.'

Despite being working class in a classless, Communist society, Gonen saw at a young age that his family was afforded special privileges by Communist Party leaders, and that he garnered undue respect from schoolmates and even the parents of his friends. Food was never an issue, and Gonen's clothing was generally newer and better than that of the other boys his age. In the summer, when other children had barely enough to eat, Gonen would slurp slices of watermelon and citrus fruit, a delicacy in 1950s Russia.

Gonen was special because his maternal grandfather ran their village's black market out of the basement of the family home. Though he was just seven years old when he saw him for the last time, Gonen has distinct memories of his Granpappa Wolf. Gonen sensed at a young age that what his grandfather did was against the rules, but he also saw Wolf as being calm and not too bothered by any potential consequences. He was the patriarch, and both his daughters lived in his home with their children. To Gonen, Wolf was larger than life. Soldiers, doctors, and other powerful people—including local Communist Party leaders—lined up outside the house to see what Wolf might have for sale. Wolf happily dispensed canned citrus fruits and tomatoes, extra rations of medicine, and whatever else he could get his hands on in exchange for cash and favours. Gonen remembers his grandfather having gold coins at a time when Russian citizens were not allowed to own gold. He recalls soldiers looking the other way when his grandfather would lug a new shipment of canning supplies into the basement of the family home.

But there was one thing Wolf could not provide—cortisone. Growing up Gonen was told that his father had contracted severe arthritis from sleeping on the ground for weeks at a time while fleeing Nazi-occupied Poland. Gonen remembers Jacob Gershman as a frail man who needed crutches to walk.

By the time Gonen was a teenager, his father was wheelchair bound. When Gonen was almost nine, Wolf decided it would be best for his daughter's family to move first to Poland, where cortisone was more readily available on the black market, and from there to Israel, which, at the time, was just a nine-year-old country but one in which cortisone could be obtained legally. Gonen's last memory of Granpappa Wolf is of standing on a train platform and being told by the man who had provided for him his entire life, 'Boy, you are going to Palestine.'

Seven years later, when they were settled in Israel, the Gershmans received word that Granpappa Wolf had fallen and died. He had, by all accounts, run his black market without penalty until the day he died.

In Israel, Gonen saw what life without bending the rules was like. The family settled in Holon, a working-class suburb of Tel Aviv. His parents worked long hours operating a lunch counter in an industrial park. His mother took a second job cleaning houses, but money was tight—from all over Europe Jews were flocking to Israel. There was a construction boom underway, but, unable to work, Gonen's father had to make money doing what he could with his debilitating condition. That amounted to sitting behind the counter of the restaurant working a cash register while his wife cooked meals.

The cortisone only did so much to curb his pain, and, in the process, Gonen's father became addicted to the drug. It would eventually kill him, causing his heart to stop. Gonen was in and out of trouble as a teenager, committing his first serious crime when he was twelve. One day after school, he convinced a schoolmate—who was, according to Gonen, 'a stupid boy'—to let him into his home. The boy's parents ran a grocery store, and after rummaging through the family's belongings, Gonen came across a box containing receipts from the store. He stole $50, and the following day he skipped school to go to Tel Aviv. Once there, he splurged on everything his parents could not afford to give him: He saw a double feature movie, gorged himself on candy, ate his first bag of cherries, and bought himself a pocket-knife.

Gonen's parents were consumed by the business, which brought in about $400 a month, plus free food for the family. Gonen never did his homework and was barely learning to read.

'And when I did read, it was cowboy magazines,' he said.

Right after his bar mitzvah a woman from the school came to visit his mother and told her flatly, 'He's never in school. The boy is a bum—he's going nowhere.' Gonen's parents made the decision to send their troubled son to a *kibbutz*.

A *kibbutz* is an Israeli collective community that combines socialism and Zionism in a form of practical Labour Zionism. In addition to having one less mouth to feed, Gonen's parents thought he would benefit from the shared labour and collective education. Instead, Gonen began hanging out with older kids, who taught him how to smoke and drink, and started his lifelong affair with marijuana and hashish. He had his first sexual experience there, with an older Romanian girl named Rena who was supposed to have been teaching him how to swim.

He spent the next few years being thrown out of one *kibbutz* after another. At one, he burgled a warehouse and stole socks and underwear; at another, he was thrown out for using hashish. Military service was compulsory for 18-year-old men in Israel, but Gonen liked the idea of getting out of Israel and seeing the world, so at 16 he forged documents to gain acceptance to the Military Cadet Academy. Successful completion of the academy would guarantee him acceptance into the naval force. Gonen excelled, and graduated first in his class.

Only when he was on the verge of being deployed did Israeli officials realise he was not old enough to join the navy. After killing time before he could legally join the navy by working as a car thief, Gonen was assigned to a ship that made stops in Europe and the Middle East. Each port of call was a party: nightclubs with thumping music, new foods, jukeboxes, and, best of all, prostitutes. Gonen estimates that in a six-week period he slept with more than 30 prostitutes who, collectively, spoke 17 different languages. From that point on, he would prefer his women with an edge—throughout the course of his life he would fall in love with women with explosive personalities who seemed to draw trouble wherever they went.

After the Six Day War in 1967, Gonen served out the rest of his three-year military service in Israel. While on leave he would typically steal a car to get from his base to Tel Aviv, then steal another car to get back to the base when his leave was over. A friend had sold him a key that would open parking meters on Tel Aviv streets. Gonen even bought brown shorts and a tan shirt to imitate the meter collectors' uniforms and would spend his days off from the military breaking into parking meters and stealing the change.

He ran into trouble, however, when a photographer taking shots of the Tel Aviv waterfront from a third-storey balcony noticed him 'working' on the street below. The photographer called the police and, after Gonen was arrested, sold the pictures to a local newspaper. He was 18. And he was going to jail.

GONEN WAS HELD in a Tel Aviv jail for 40 days before the charges against him were dropped. He stuck firm to the story that he had found the key to the parking meters. When asked about the six stolen cars that had turned up with his fingerprints, he claimed that he had had the unfortunate luck of being picked up hitchhiking by six different car thieves. Even after he was beaten by his interrogators—first with fists and, later, with a phone book—Gonen refused to rat out the friend who had sold him the parking meter key. That refusal gained Gonen respect when he was returned, bruised and bloody, to the general jail population after each day's round of questioning. Normally, an 18-year-old in jail would be prey for older inmates, but Gonen soon gained their affection. They called him 'the soldier' and laughed when someone started circulating the newspaper photo of Gonen breaking into the parking meters.

Gonen was struck by the fact that none of the men seemed too concerned that they were in jail. They weren't worried and seemed to enjoy the camaraderie. He met men he had read about in the police logs of the newspaper. He befriended Yehezkel Aslan, who had started life as a poor Iraqi immigrant in Tel Aviv's Hatvka Quarter but would rise to become one of the country's biggest importers of heroin. By the time he was gunned down in 1993, many in Tel Aviv's slums saw Aslan as a Robin Hood figure, noting that he had donated money to build a treatment facility for heroin addicts, as well as money for a professional soccer team. His funeral was attended by thousands of poor Israelis. A detective investigating the murder, who said he normally felt no remorse for the victims of gangland slayings, told Israeli newspapers, 'This time it's different. We've grown up with Aslan.'

There was only one other inmate in Gonen's age range who didn't get harassed by the older prisoners. Johnny Attias was 16 and commanded even more respect than Gonen. Attias was five feet seven inches tall and scrawny, but he was fearless. Older criminals would enlist him to assault inmates who had crossed them. Even at 16 Attias was getting used to spending long stretches in solitary confinement. He was a northern African Jew, and he had unusual bluish-green eyes that stood in stark contrast to his dark complexion. When he wasn't in the hole, he and Gonen traded cigarettes and talked about scams they could pull once they were released.

It would be nearly 20 years before he saw Attias again in New York City. After 40 days, Gonen was released to his father's custody. Gonen helped the old man onto the bus for the ride back to Holon. His father cried.

After he was discharged from the navy, Gonen got a job as a heavy machine operator. But he still found ways to make his parents cry. His mother would get upset every time she saw her son come home with a new car, a new suit, or a new watch. She knew he was earning meagre wages. She knew he was still stealing.

Gonen was good at being a criminal. He had been told as much by Sammy Merckel, an Israeli who lived in Munich and came to Tel Aviv a few times each year on holiday. Merckel had met Gonen in a bar the previous summer and had been impressed with some of the burglary jobs Gonen had been able to pull off on his own. Merckel also gave Gonen a lecture about robbing from Israelis. He told Gonen he should move to Munich, where American GIs stationed in the still-reconstructing country refused to deal with German nationals and, as a result, gave all their black market business to Jews.

'Why would you want to steal from your own people when you can steal from *them*?' Merckel said.

Merckel was right. Beyond that, Gonen knew if another of his arrests was written up in the Israeli papers, his parents would likely die from shame and heartbreak. On 2 January 1970, Gonen walked into a café in Munich that Merckel had said he liked to hang out in. Gonen had stolen $18,000 in jewels a few days earlier. It was the biggest score of his life and gave him not only the money, but also the reason he needed to get out of Israel. Gonen knew Merckel was a master safe cracker who ran a crew. He knew that Merckel wouldn't just give him lots of work—he'd give him an education.

Sammy Merckel was sipping a drink at the end of the bar, as if he had been waiting for Gonen all those months—as if he knew Gonen would show up.

'What took you so long?' Sammy Merckel said.

GONEN STILL HAS a photo of himself, taken a few months after he arrived in Germany. He is standing in the Tilbori, a famous Munich nightclub in the late 1960s and early 1970s. He is not yet 22 years old, but he glares with the self-confidence of someone twice his age. He is well dressed, wearing a designer button-down shirt open at the neck and a sports coat draped over his shoulders. While doctors, lawyers, and politicians undoubtedly had to wait hours to get into the Tilbori that night, Gonen had just as undoubtedly cruised to the front of the long line, warmly greeted the bouncers, and strolled into the club.

Germany is where Gonen became a career criminal and got a taste of the respect and power being a gangster would afford him. Sammy Merckel taught him everything he needed to know about the lifestyle, from casing out jobs to cracking safes to fencing stolen goods. It was not a flawless education—Gonen would be sentenced to prison twice during the eight years he spent in Germany—but by the time he left Munich in 1978, he would be unable to think of any other kind of life.

Gonen learned quickly, despite some setbacks. On one of his first jobs—stealing *Fiddler on the Roof* ticket receipts at the Deutsche Theatre in Munich—a team of security guards had swarmed in when Gonen's inexperienced lookout man got spooked and ran off. Trying not to get caught, Gonen jumped from a third-storey roof and shattered his right ankle. It was an injury that would give him discomfort for the rest of his life. He had to drive home, operating the clutch, brake, and gas pedals with his left foot and crashing his car through a column of a dozen security guards to avoid arrest. But, as Merckel noted when he went to visit Gonen in the hospital, he had done the most important thing: He hadn't gotten caught.

As a criminal, Gonen's talents were considerable. In Germany he would become an expert document forger. He had solid instincts for scouting out a robbery target and putting together a job. And on the job, few were better. Merckel had called him a natural safe cracker, and unlike other young criminals he had imported from Israel to Germany in the late 1960s and early 1970s, Gonen kept it together on a job.

'In the movies, you'll see a guy take a shot of whiskey before he goes on a job,' Merckel said. 'That doesn't happen in real life, but you do see people get sick. I had one guy who got diarrhoea every time we'd go on a job. We'd be getting ready to open the safe and he'd be looking for someplace to take a shit.'

But not Gonen.

Gonen started dating his first wife shortly after he started to carve out a reputation for himself in Munich. Doris Calle was beautiful, statuesque with soft red hair. She was eight years older than Gonen but took an immediate liking to the boy the other gangsters called 'the Young Turk.' Calle was also a hustler; nightclub managers would hire Calle and her friends to bring travelling businessmen into the clubs. The girls would get the men to order an expensive string of drinks, watered-down top-shelf liquors and, if they were lucky, a bottle of champagne. A good hustler like Calle could easily make $500 in a night. By day, Calle was a frighteningly skilled shoplifter.

In 1971, the younger brother of a friend called Gonen to a jewellery store he had broken into. He asked Gonen to evaluate which merchandise to keep and which to leave behind. Gonen arrived at the store—followed shortly by the police. He would be sentenced to twenty-one months in jail. He used his time in prison to learn both English and German, and Calle remained loyal to him throughout his stint. She smuggled in cigarettes, smoked meats, cheeses, chocolates, whiskey, and other creature comforts. She also brought blank postcards from different European cities she had visited. Gonen would fill out the postcards, and the next time Calle was in Paris, Milan, or wherever the postcard had come from, she would mail it to his parents to explain his long absences between visits.

In 1972, Gonen lied to German prison officials and said he was related to one of the Israelis who had been killed at the Munich Olympic Games. It was enough to get him released from prison on the condition that he would be deported to Israel and would never return to Germany.

Gonen followed the stipulations of his release for nearly six months before he met Ran Ephraim, who helped him return to Munich.

WHEN GONEN RETURNED to Israel, he got a job managing a dive bar called Las Vegas. By day, he broke into hotel rooms, constantly paranoid of getting caught and disgracing his parents. A friend had been promoted to head security at the Ramada and had given Gonen a master key to all the rooms.

He would call Gonen at the bar when a wealthy couple left one of the hotel's suites and tell him which room was empty and how long he suspected its occupants to be out. Las Vegas was the kind of bar that attracted gangsters and lowlifes. It was the kind of place where Gonen could put up a legitimate front but still be close to the criminal element that had now become the driving force in his life. Gonen *loved* stealing, and he loved being a gangster. He hated being back in Tel Aviv and considered it just a matter of time before he'd rejoin Merckel and the rest of the crew, and return to the life he loved so much back in Munich.

Gonen and Ephraim met at Las Vegas. Ephraim was a customer and told Gonen he was in the import-export business. Gonen said he ran the bar. Both knew the other wasn't being totally forthcoming.

'Gangsters know other gangsters,' Gonen said. 'You have a way of knowing when someone is like you.' Even now, Gonen says on more than one occasion he has been able to pick out another ward of the programme while out on the town in the nameless city he now calls home.

Over the next eight years, Gonen and Ephraim would occasionally partner on jobs. In addition to smuggling stolen goods into Israel, Ephraim was also developing a reputation for smuggling people into the country, which had strict immigration controls. He would occasionally use Gonen's skills as a forger to draw up phoney documents for people who paid him tens of thousands of dollars for the chance to enter Israel.

Their first job together helped Gonen get back to Germany so he could be reunited with his fiancée and friends. Ephraim supplied Gonen with silencers for pistols, which Gonen was able to sell in Austria. The money partially staked his return to Munich.

In hindsight, Gonen's return to Germany was ill advised. He and Doris Calle finally got married and he continued to learn the ins and outs of being an art and jewel thief, but the return trip landed Gonen in prison for a second time.

In 1976, Gonen was living in Munich with Calle and running burglary jobs with Frantz, another young thief he had met through Merckel. Their specialty was safe cracking. They worked the underworld grapevine to find out when certain jewellers would be on vacation and devised complex plans to break into their homes, where many were known to keep a significant chunk of their inventory. When they came across a safe that was too difficult to crack, they would move it into a waiting truck and take it back to the garage of Gonen's flat, where they could work without interruption and with a set of bulkier but more sophisticated tools. The system worked well—until one morning, when the garage caught on fire.

It was not a serious fire—just some rags smouldering in a corner—and if Gonen had been awake, he might have been able to put it out before someone else called the fire department.

The fire fighters responding to the call had their curiosity piqued by the blowtorches, picks, and safecracker's tools that were in the smouldering garage. The fire was not serious, but when police were called, it was clear that Gonen was in serious trouble. A search of his apartment revealed jewellery that had been reported stolen. When he was fingerprinted, an Interpol background check showed that Gonen wasn't even supposed to be in the country in the first place.

Gonen's second stretch in a German prison would have been as uneventful as the first if he hadn't decided to lead a prison break. For most of the time he was there, a wing of the penitentiary was undergoing renovations. One afternoon, when the construction workers had gone on their lunch break, Gonen and three other prisoners noticed that they hadn't sealed a hole they had cut into the wall. They could see the woods across a field adjacent to the prison—woods in which they could hide until the search was called off and Gonen could get in touch with Frantz and Calle to scuttle them off to safety.

Without hesitation, Gonen bolted through the hole, as did the three other men—two Italians and a German. When they were 100 yards away from the prison, they heard shouting and alarms behind them. When they were 200 yards from the prison, they ran in separate directions into the woods. Once in the woods, Gonen felt an intense pain in his ankle—the old *Fiddler on the Roof* injury had decided to act up. At 400 yards, he could run no further. He buried himself under some brush, but two hours later search dogs swarmed his location. When he was returned to the prison, he learned that the other three men had been captured as well.

Despite the jailbreak, Gonen had no additional time added to his prison term. When he was released, he decided to follow the orders of German prison officials to never return to Germany.

IN 1980, GONEN moved to London and set up an import-export company as a front for a complex fraud ring. In its simplest form, Gonen bought expensive imported wines, golf clubs, designer clothes, and other luxury items on credit, then immediately resold them at cut rates to Greek gangsters and other underworld operatives throughout Europe and the Middle East. The scheme was designed to eventually fail. Once creditors got wise to the fact that they would never be paid, the whole operation would collapse. When it finally did collapse, Gonen fled to Guatemala, where he spent the next several months posing as an Israeli intelligence officer and operating an electronics store in

Guatemala City. He had chosen the country because it did not have an extradition treaty with Great Britain.

He was still married to Doris Calle, but she was back in Europe, so he started dating a woman named Julia. Julia's father was a famous general and the brother of the president elect in a country on the verge of a civil war. By December 1981, officials started to ask questions about Gonen—they had figured out that his intelligence officer persona was just a front. Julia arranged for an emergency visa for Gonen to spend ten days in New York City before returning to Israel.

'Things are just too dangerous for you right now,' Julia said.

'People are asking questions. They know you're not what they thought you were. Come back when things are safer.'

He fled Guatemala just after dawn, and by the time he landed in Miami for a layover, armed members of Iximche, a counterinsurgency death squad, had been to Julia's house asking to speak with Gonen. When he landed in New York and called Julia, he learned that officials had seized the $80,000 in his bank account and the entire inventory of his electronics store in Guatemala City. Gonen knew he would never return to Guatemala.

'Get an abortion,' he told Julia, who was three months pregnant with his child.

Gonen spent those ten days in New York sleeping on the couch of a friend of a friend, a cab driver named Morty who spent most of his free time at the famed Chelsea Hotel.

'Where are we going?' Gonen asked in the off-duty cab Morty had borrowed for Gonen's first night in Manhattan.

'A funeral.'

'A funeral?' Gonen said.

'More like a party than a funeral,' Morty said. 'But a funeral. You'll like it.'

The funeral was for a lesser-known resident of the Chelsea Hotel, home to an eclectic mix of writers, musicians, artists, and wannabes. As Gonen would see the instant he walked into the lobby, the hotel's slogan— 'A rest stop for rare individuals'—was fitting. Its residents have included Dylan Thomas, William Burroughs, Bob Dylan, Andy Warhol, Janis Joplin, Arthur Miller, Jackson Pollack, Patti Smith, Sid Vicious, and eventually Ron Gonen, although he knew none of this on that cold December night.

Gonen was dressed in a tailored suit and looked conservative in comparison to most of the other people in the lobby who wore loud colours, revealing clothing, or both. But on that night—given that 24 hours earlier he had barely escaped a Central American country with his life—he might have been rarer than all of them.

At the party, Gonen recounted his story to Rita Fecher, a resident and artist who was best known among the Chelsea's residents for her cartoon like depiction of the building, which included portraits of the hotel's residents in each of the windows.

Fecher had been a South Bronx schoolteacher who would later produce a documentary that featured interviews with her students taken in the late 1960s.

She portrayed herself as an artist who dealt a little pot. But the more Gonen talked with her, the more he realised she was a drug dealer who did a little art.

Business was good in a place like the Chelsea, where residents consumed Fecher's pot and hallucinogenic drugs by the pound. She even offered Gonen the bag of marijuana from which she had expertly rolled a joint. Gonen estimated the bag had a street value of $300. For Fecher, it was a small price to pay to listen to Gonen's Guatemalan adventures.

'And that's just the past nine months,' Gonen said. 'My whole life has been, well, interesting.'

She invited him back. For the next week, Gonen spent most afternoons in the Chelsea. He talked with Fecher, smoked pot, drank, and watched the people who came and went. Gonen was instantly curious about one particular group.

They were well-dressed men—they were always men—and their visits were never more than a few minutes long. Whichever resident they came to visit was happy—if not outright relieved—to see them. They conducted hushed transactions in the corner of the lobby or behind the closed door of an apartment, and they left just as inconspicuously as they had arrived.

'Who's that guy?' Gonen said to Fecher, nodding toward one of these men on his third afternoon at the Chelsea.

'Him? Coke dealer,' Fecher said.

'Why don't they just buy it from you?'

'I don't deal coke,' she said. 'Too much of a hassle. The problem with New York is everyone jacks the price up without knowing what they're buying. So they're paying $120 for a gram of rat poison.'

Gonen chuckled.

'If you really wanted to make money,' Fecher said, 'you'd find a way to sell good coke at a good price. You'd run every one of these guys out of business.'

For Gonen, being a criminal meant respect. Gonen wanted easy money and unlimited respect. The 1970s showed him that crime, while it had its inherent risks, was the way for someone like him to get that money and respect. Indeed, he had lost a few years of his life to a German jail cell, but he also had all his toes and fingers and more money than any of the people he had gone to grade school with.

Gonen was intelligent and had an entrepreneurial mind. And when he saw the coke dealers coming in and out of the lobby of the Chelsea Hotel, when he saw the respect their presence drew and the money they collected, Gonen wanted to be a coke dealer. Gonen called nightclub owners and underworld associates in Tel Aviv and found out that there, as in New York, cocaine was the emerging black market commodity.

Being a cocaine dealer—particularly a cocaine dealer who planned to operate out of the Middle East—was not an easy proposition in 1982. Today, cocaine trafficking is a multibillion-dollar industry, albeit an illicit one, with established supply lines and free market controls. In 1982, there were few established supply lines, the quality of the product varied from week to week, and, most troubling of all, the price fluctuated widely. Cocaine dealers needed a potent and inexpensive product that would get users hooked in short order.

At first, Gonen took expensive trips to Amsterdam to buy cocaine in quantities of a couple of dozen grams from glorified street dealers. It was a safe amount to take on the train back to Brussels and then on his flight back to Tel Aviv. But each gram could cost as much as $50 or $60 and only retailed for $75 in the nightclubs where Gonen was operating. One trip might yield a nearly pure product, but another might yield cocaine cut so many times with kerosene and other agents that users would get bloody noses or, even worse, not feel the effects of the high.

Gonen, however, quickly rose from cheap nightclub dealer to the dealer of choice in cities on two continents. And much of that rapid rise can be attributed to Ran Ephraim.

BEFORE RON GONEN could really help Ran Ephraim, Ephraim had to convince Gonen to move to the United States permanently.

'Why even bother going back to Tel Aviv?' Ephraim said one afternoon, after Mango had left the motel room in Los Angeles and Gonen had bemoaned the long flight that he would be taking after a few days at the Chelsea Hotel.

Gonen did not hesitate. 'Doris,' he said.

At 40, Doris Calle was eight years older than Gonen, but she still had the statuesque beauty that stunned crowds at Munich nightclubs in the early 1970s. She and Gonen had been maintaining a long-distance marriage for several years. When he had been operating in London, Calle was living in Paris, and they would see each other on weekends.

It was no secret that Gonen cheated on Calle during his long stretches away from home. He hadn't told her about Julia, but Calle was smart enough to know that Gonen hadn't been faithful while he was in Central America. And while Gonen had initially been angry that Calle spent so much of his money while he was away, that anger dissipated as his small cocaine empire gained ground. On most days, Gonen seemed genuinely happy to be back in Tel Aviv, living with his wife.

'I need to tell you something about Doris,' Ephraim said.

'And you're not going to like it.'

Doris Calle was a close friend with Ephraim's ex-wife, Mickey, who was still living in Tel Aviv. They saw each other daily, and Ephraim got updates on how Calle was doing when Mickey called him to complain that he was late in sending her money.

'Doris and Mickey are pretty tight,' Ephraim said. 'Doris has been seeing someone since you left for London.'

That had been more than a year ago. He was a straight guy, Ephraim said, a civilian who probably didn't know what he was getting into when he hooked up with a woman like Calle. But he knew all about Gonen, and he was terrified.

'He keeps hearing about Doris' husband, the gangster,' Ephraim said. 'He's afraid, but he's also pissed because he sees a lot less of her now that you're back in Tel Aviv.'

Gonen's anger flared, but it was tempered by thoughts of his own infidelity. It only made sense that she had given up on him.

'Fuck it,' Gonen said.

'Fuck it? You got bigger problems than that,' Ephraim said.

'He's been telling people he's going to go to the cops. He's going to tell them that you're dealing to get you put away. He doesn't have the balls or know how to kill you, but he can do the next best thing.'

Gonen felt betrayed. No matter how tough times had been with Calle, she had never let outsiders in on his criminal activities.

'But if New York is as good as you say it is, why take the risk?' Ephraim said. 'We could make a lot more money if you were there full time.'

Gonen replayed their conversation over in his mind on the five-hour flight from Los Angeles to New York. When he checked into the Chelsea, he told the staff he would be staying for a few days and returning the following week. When he returned, Gonen said, he would need long-stay accommodations. That afternoon he traded cocaine for the cash his friends had collected during his week away. A few days later, he flew back to Tel Aviv with $25,000 and 200 grams of cocaine, and gave Doris Calle half of the money as soon as he arrived at her apartment.

'This is for you and your new boyfriend. No hard feelings, as long as he knows how to keep his mouth shut,' he said. 'I'm leaving. I'm going to New York and I'm not coming back.'

2

SPARKLE PLENTY

Ron Gonen wanted to swing.

Long before he arrived in New York City in December 1981, Gonen had heard all about the swingers' clubs that dominated the city's seedier side in the pre-HIV days of the late 1970s and early 1980s. They were all-night, couples-only orgies for the uninhibited. The most famous clubs were on the Upper East Side and weren't really clubs at all, but apartments that had been designed for carefree sex: endless reels of pornographic movies playing in one room, every inch of available floor space covered with mattresses in another, and mirrored ceilings in a third.

Doormen charged a modest fee—no more than $100 per couple—but only the seediest clubs would admit single men. And that was Gonen's dilemma: He was suddenly single, but he didn't dare ask any of the more refined women he had met through his growing cocaine trade to accompany him to a swingers' club.

He called Alexander Algor.

'You need to give me the number of a woman who will go to a swingers' club with me,' Gonen said. 'She doesn't have to fuck me. I don't care if she walks out as soon as they let us in. I just need to get in the door.'

It was no surprise to Algor that Gonen wanted to go to a swingers' club. Since Gonen had formalised his separation from his wife, he had been out of control in his lustful pursuits. On more than one occasion, Algor had called a woman he was dating only to hear Gonen's voice in the background. It seemed as soon as Algor introduced a woman to Gonen—even if he made it clear that he was romantically interested in the woman—Gonen would sleep with her. Algor, thinking he would get a little bit of payback on his friend, flipped through his address book and stopped at a number he hadn't called in months.

'I know just the person,' Algor said, then gave Gonen the phone number for Honey Tesman.

'HE PROBABLY FIGURED we'd drive each other crazy and kill each other,' Tesman said when she recalled their first meeting.

'Alex was mad at me for breaking his heart, and he was mad at Ron for stealing all of his girlfriends.'

Tesman had dated Algor. Tesman had dated a lot of men.

By the time Gonen called in June 1982, she was 32, divorced, and, at the time, engaged to three other men. Her long list of previous boyfriends contained powerful and, in many cases, ruined New York men. She had had a long-term relationship with Tony Sirico, the mobster who would go on to star as a caricature of his real life persona in *The Sopranos* and Mafia movies. She dated vice presidents of Columbia Records and Guess? Jeans, hit men, lounge singers, professional athletes, and—her favourite type of boyfriend—cocaine dealers. Her boyfriend at the time, a high-profile head of an advertising agency, was old and boring and rich. He had given Tesman a job, which was more to say he had given her a pay cheque and an office she could show up to in her pyjamas to wait out the effects of the previous night's party. In return, she had given him a freebase cocaine addiction.

Honey Tesman had been thrown out of more high schools and dropped out of more colleges than she could remember. She had a daughter from her first marriage, but, because of her explosive personality, the ten-year-old girl lived with Tesman's more stable family members on Long Island. She had shot an ex-boyfriend in the leg over an imagined dispute. Another time, when one of her gangster boyfriends got involved with the Lufthansa heist made famous in the movie Goodfellas, Tesman's car had been fire bombed.

'Your daughter might want to rethink the people she spends her time with,' the police officer who was sent to file the report on the burned-out car told her mother.

When she was a teenager, a doctor had diagnosed her with 'arrested development,' telling Tesman's mother 'She's stuck at two years old. She likes being two years old. She doesn't *want* to grow up, and she *isn't* going to grow up.'

Life hadn't always been so chaotic. Honey Tesman was the youngest of three daughters, each born seven years apart, in a tight-knit Jewish family. Her mother tended to the girls' schooling, even vowing to work cleaning toilets if she needed to help pay for their college educations. She wouldn't need to. Her husband owned a successful dry-cleaning plant that serviced most of the cleaners on Long Island and the outer boroughs.

Roberta, the oldest, would become a teacher and marry a psychologist. Paula would marry the owner of a successful chain of locksmith stores. Honey would be the first student expelled from her high school for smoking pot.

But it didn't matter—Honey Tesman would always have a special place in her father's heart. On the day she was born with a full head of black curls, her father—a diehard Dick Tracy fan—bounded into the family's Long Beach house and told Paula and Roberta, 'Your mother just gave birth to Sparkle Plenty,' a reference to the comic strip character's beautiful girlfriend.

Honey's bedroom—the biggest—was at the front of the house. The family lived on a quiet, tree-lined residential street, but when Honey was seven, she began staying up at night to protect her family from 'the visitor.' She never saw the visitor, only the long shadow the ominous man cast on the ceiling of her bedroom.

'I was going to stay up all night and protect my family until he went away,' Honey said. 'But he never went away.'

Honey never told her parents or her sisters about the visitor. It would be years later—and long after her doctor prescribed Seconal to help Honey sleep—that she and her mother determined that the shadow didn't come from an unwanted visitor but from an old suit of her father's that hung near a window of an adjoining room.

Seconal is a barbiturate used as a sedative and hypnotic. It is now used sparingly, but in the 1950s, doctors would regularly prescribe it to children who had trouble sleeping. The problem was that it didn't help Honey sleep.

'It got me high and I liked it,' Honey said. 'I wasn't going to go to sleep and lose that feeling.'

When Honey Tesman told Gonen that she had been high since she was seven years old, she wasn't exaggerating.

AT FIRST THEY hated each other.

Gonen was a brash cocaine dealer, new on the Manhattan scene, and had been calling her for the past six weeks. She wouldn't always call him back, but she often missed him when he was away on one of his frequent trips to Tel Aviv in early 1982. When he finally showed up at the office where Tesman was working for her boyfriend, she made Gonen wait in the lavish reception area outside her office.

When she did work, Tesman could be a very good saleswoman. She'd bypass the low-level ad buyers in charge of purchasing print campaigns and call the secretary of the chief executive directly.

'Tell him his Honey is calling,' she would coo into the phone.

Often the flustered secretary would forward the call straight through to her boss to avoid the red-faced exchange of a telephone message from a perceived mistress. Once she had the confused CEO on the line, Honey would flirt through the line, and more than one Fortune 500 company bought an expensive—and unnecessary—ad campaign.

Gonen didn't know any of this. All he knew was that he was killing more than an hour thumbing through magazines. For months he had tried to date Tesman, and now she would only meet him in her office and only after he had grown thoroughly aggravated in the waiting room.

But when she emerged from her office, Gonen's anger melted. She still had the head of black curls and penetrating eyes. Her body was tight, and Gonen sensed that if there was any woman in New York who could keep up with his frantic pace, Tesman was it. He didn't hesitate to join her and another man for dinner that evening.

What Gonen didn't know was that the man, who picked them up at her office in a brand new Mercedes, thought that *he* was Tesman's boyfriend.

Later that evening, when the soon-to-be ex-boyfriend was drunk and tired of the flirting between Gonen and Tesman, he rammed the Mercedes into an embankment on Lexington Avenue in Manhattan. He later said he was hoping to kill—or at least seriously injure—all three of them.

On their second date, Honey Tesman took Gonen to a restaurant in Little Italy. The owner came to their table and kissed Tesman on the cheek, then smiled warmly as he shook Gonen's hand.

'That's Vinny, my ex-boyfriend,' Tesman said after the man had walked away. 'He's going to poison your food. He's very jealous.'

She had said it so matter-of-factly that Gonen thought she was joking. The next morning he called to tell her he had been up all night with a severe case of diarrhoea.

But if Honey Tesman didn't destroy him and if one of her ex-boyfriends didn't kill him, then Gonen saw potential in their relationship, at least in a business sense. In between car wrecks and tainted dinners, she led him through a string of hip New York City nightclubs. She seemed to know everybody in the clubs, from the wealthy, pretentious patrons to the jazz musicians who sweated on stage into the Manhattan dawn. They all greeted her with a hug and a kiss and many would whisper into her ear: 'Got anything?'

Gonen had been giving Tesman cocaine since the first day they met, and, like he did for all his new clients, he never asked for money up front. Tesman's appetite for the drug, however, exceeded all of his other clients. She routinely kept an ounce loose in her purse and, whenever the need arose, would use a solid silver straw a friend had purchased at Tiffany's to take a quick hit.

So when Honey Tesman offered excuses as to why she didn't have money, Gonen wasn't surprised.

'We were taking the boat to Fire Island,' Tesman would say. 'We were sitting on the deck and when I opened the bag, it all blew away.'

Gonen knew she was lying, but it didn't matter. While she was tearing through a half kilo a month on her own, she was introducing him to dozens of clients who would purchase that much product in a week. Tesman was quickly becoming overhead for Gonen, but in return he was introduced to clients he never would have met otherwise. And they were the right clientele, the upper middle-class types, the people who had six-figure salaries or trust funds and not much else to do in their free time outside of self-destruction.

If anyone could handle Honey Tesman, it was Ron Gonen. Or so he thought.

AS HE CONTINUED to court Tesman, Gonen grew obsessed with the quality of his cocaine.

'The last thing I need,' he said, 'is some model standing on a runway with a bloody nose because of my product.'

Even cocaine of average quality would not suffice for people who demanded top quality in everything they purchased, be it wristwatches or narcotics. What Gonen really wanted was a steady supply of the best cocaine at the best price, and the more he learned about the Gotham market, the more he realised the transcontinental trips to see Ran Ephraim weren't helping him meet any of those goals.

It wasn't just that Ran Ephraim's cocaine was of only slightly above-average quality. And it wasn't because Gonen was starting to dread the cross-country flights—on the contrary, he sometimes enjoyed getting away from Tesman's frantic pace. It had more to do with how Gonen had been trained as a criminal.

Dating back to his time in Germany, Gonen had prided himself on being an independent gangster. In

Munich, Sammy Merckel—his criminal mentor—had shown him how to break into buildings, crack safes, and deal with fences, but he had also stressed that Gonen needed to break out on his own and not get too close to anyone.

Sometimes, particularly when he was young and inexperienced, being independent had had disastrous consequences. But not relying on others usually served him well; if one fence wanted to short him on the price for a rare painting or a gaudy set of jewels, Gonen could go on to the next fence. And if an underworld accomplice got pinched, he wouldn't know Gonen well enough to trade information for a reduced sentence.

Of course, Merckel had also warned him to stay away from the drug trade, saying it was reserved for a lower class of criminal, but Gonen had conveniently ignored that bit of wisdom since arriving in the United States.

Gonen needed Ran Ephraim, but he also needed half a dozen other suppliers who were capable of delivering quality product on a consistent basis. If Ephraim hit a dry patch or, even worse, if Ephraim got busted, Gonen's business could be shut down in a matter of hours.

'IT'S GOOD, BUT it's not great,' Tesman would inevitably say after she sampled Ephraim's latest batch from Los Angeles.

'You really need to try Spencer's blow.'

Gonen had met Spencer a few times and had sampled his cocaine when Honey Tesman was in the mood to share. Spencer was a fixture at Tesman's favourite jazz clubs, a soundman who had made live recordings of everyone from the Gil Evans Orchestra to Chaka Kahn.

'You mean Black Kojak?' Gonen said, referring to Spencer's dark skin and shaved head. 'Why don't you take me over to his place so I can talk with him?'

'I can't do that,' Honey said. 'I owe him money. Something like $3,000.'

Spencer, a Vietnam vet in his late 40s, was an intimidating presence behind the soundboards of the nightclubs he frequented. He was rumoured to be importing five kilos of cocaine straight from Peru each month and had a reputation for not tolerating the presence of people who owed him money. He was a likable guy, but Gonen could see why Tesman would be worried about bumping into him with such a large debt.

'Call him up,' Gonen said. 'I'll take care of whatever you owe him.'

Spencer lived in an East Village loft that took up an entire floor of a converted warehouse. The industrial elevator took Tesman and Gonen to a dimly lit alcove, and, when the elevator gate pulled back, all that was before them was a thick steel door, the kind one was more apt to find on a loading dock than in the threshold of a luxurious loft apartment. Tesman rapped on the door.

A set of eyes peeked through a slot in the gate. Gonen heard a series of locks, chains, and dead bolts being undone inside. The door slid up, and there stood Spencer, hands on his hips with his immaculate loft spread out behind him. There were tens of thousands of dollars of sound recording equipment neatly arranged on one side of the apartment, and stylish furniture spread out on the other.

'Do you have my money?' Spencer said to Tesman without acknowledging Gonen.

'He does,' Tesman said. 'Do you have any blow?'

As a question, it was an understatement. In the kitchen, that had obviously never been used for cooking, were all the makings of a cocaine department store. Five kilos, each individually packaged into plastic sausage casings like the ones found in any New York City deli, were stacked neatly on the counter. A sixth was open, its contents partially spilled out onto a table. Next to the table was a massive stainless steel machine that looked as if it had been pillaged from a bakery, down to the thin layer of white powder that covered its surface.

Before Spencer could complete the lengthy process of reaffixing the padlocks, dead bolts, and chains, there was another rap on the door. 'Fucking hell,' Spencer said as he undid the locks and let in a well-dressed man. The man, who Gonen guessed was in his twenties, would be the first of three visitors Spencer would service in the short time Gonen and Tesman were in his loft.

Gonen settled Tesman's tab, which was closer to $4,000 than the 'something like $3,000' she had said. Spencer served another client, then gave Gonen a quick tour. The machine on the kitchen table, he explained, was used for cutting cocaine with inert agents.

'Everyone thinks cocaine makes you have to take a shit,' Spencer said. 'It's not the cocaine—it's the laxatives people use to cut it.'

The cocaine that went in one end was as pure as it had been on the day it was processed in Peru; when the cocaine came out the other end, it was packaged in the neat, kilo bricks that Gonen was more accustomed to seeing. It was also less pure—but still more potent than anything Ran Ephraim could deliver. As an added bonus, Spencer didn't use laxatives to cut his coke, instead opting for a more expensive chemical compound that was sold in head shops.

'So are you going to sell me the cocaine on that end of the machine or *that* end of the machine?' Gonen joked, pointing to the pure product.

'From what I hear, I should sell you anything you want,' Spencer said. 'Honey says you have a talent for moving product.'

Gonen told Spencer he would pay him in cash, up front, and that he would never ask for or accept credit. In return Spencer would make sure their transactions would be done in private; there would be no low-level dealers stopping by like the three who had already been in the loft that evening to catch a glimpse of Gonen.

'They say you're bringing in five keys a month,' Gonen said.

'That sounds about right,' Spencer said.

'You better order more,' Gonen said, 'or you won't have any left to sell to anyone else.'

BY FEBRUARY 1983, Gonen had made good on his promise to purchase five kilos of cocaine from Spencer each month. But it wasn't enough. He had a second connection in Miami and was networking with drug smugglers and Dominican gangsters who were working out of Spanish Harlem.

At the same time, his list of retail customers was growing. Gonen was developing a niche among the affluent New Yorkers who were picking up the new and deadly trend. And that niche was being carved in large part because of Honey Tesman. She introduced him to hairdressers on Long Island who dealt small quantities to bored housewives. New Jersey mobsters, after decades of resisting the drug trade, were happy to meet Gonen. In turn the Mafiosos introduced Gonen to construction workers on Mob-controlled jobs, and they, too, seemed to be more than willing to dump half a pay cheque in Gonen's pocket. Doormen at nightclubs, from the punk rock bastion CBGB to the more refined Upper East Side jazz clubs, all knew Gonen by name.

Gonen never presented himself as a dealer. Instead he liked to be portrayed as a well-connected guy who could always get quality cocaine at a relatively decent price. To ease the paranoia of potential clients, he would occasionally do a line, and he always sampled any product he planned to purchase. But he didn't do it enough to be classified even as a social user, and addiction never entered his mind.

Until one night.

'Try this,' Tesman said, offering Gonen her well-used freebase pipe. The pipe was made of glass and warm to the touch from Tesman's constant use.

Gonen had been drinking. He had been hounding Tesman for months to slow down on her cocaine use, which now amounted to several ounces every week. There are a little bit more than 28 grams in an ounce, and a social user might use a gram or two over the course of a Saturday night. Honey Tesman used a gram or two for breakfast.

But it was the freebasing, the act of cooking the cocaine into a rock that could then be smoked in a glass pipe like Tesman's, that bothered him the most. The high, he had been told, was even more intense and more instantaneous than snorting, and freebasers were the lowest of all addicts.

'Are you fucking kidding me?' Gonen said, eyeing the pipe.

'You're such a fucking hypocrite,' Tesman said angrily. 'It's *fun*, Ron. You're making all this money and working all the time. Just have fun for once.'

He glared at her, but was distracted by the ringing telephone. It was Ran Ephraim.

Ephraim had been calling daily for the past week, and until that night Gonen had been able to duck his calls. Everyone—from his retail clients to his suppliers in New York and Miami—was happy with Gonen's growing empire. That is, everyone but Ran Ephraim. Ran Ephraim was miserable. Every connection Gonen made in New York, every purchase made at the 10th Street Baths, the Bowery, or in his apartment at the

Chelsea Hotel was money coming out of Ephraim's pocket.

'What? Is business bad?' Ephraim said without saying 'Hello.'

'No,' Gonen slipped. 'Business is fine.'

'Either business is bad, or you're cutting me out,' Ephraim hissed. 'Either business is bad or you're fucking me.'

Gonen explained the risk involved and the quality of the product he was purchasing in New York. He explained that it was Ephraim's supplier, Mango, and not Gonen who was short-changing Ephraim. By the time Mango brought the cocaine to Los Angeles, it was not nearly as pure as the cocaine Gonen bought in Miami or from Spencer for the same price or less. He described his growing retail trade, and how every time he spent two days flying to and from Los Angeles, it was two lost selling days.

'I'm taking over. I sell it as quick as I buy it, and flying to Los Angeles isn't quick enough,' Gonen said. 'Besides, it's too risky. Ending up in jail because I get caught on a plane with half a kilo taped to my chest isn't going to help me.'

Ephraim was silent for a moment.

'Fine,' he finally said. 'If New York is as good as you say it is I'm moving there.'

Gonen stammered, trying to find a way to keep Ephraim in Los Angeles without resuming the gruelling schedule of flying there several times a month. But Ephraim cut him off.

'I'll see you in a week.'

Gonen was visibly tense as he set the telephone receiver into its cradle. Tesman looked up from the kitchen table where she was cooking another batch of cocaine.

'What?' she said. 'What is it?'

'We may have a problem.'

After Gonen had explained Ephraim's impending arrival, after he had explained the hand holding Ephraim would need and his attitude of always taking care of himself first, Tesman once again offered the pipe to Gonen.

'*Try* this.'

And for the first time in the eight months they had been dating, Gonen did not resist. He did not fight her, just took the pipe with a blank expression on his face and inhaled deeply as Tesman held the propane lighter to the pipe's opening. The rocks in the bowl crackled, and chemical-flavoured smoke shot into Gonen's lungs.

Gonen eased back into the sofa they were sitting on. His Ran Ephraim problem went away, if only for an evening.

GONEN HAD ALWAYS had an addictive personality. He was a lifelong hashish user and smoked cigarettes constantly. He was addicted to stealing, robbing, and getting one over on the system.

He loved to gamble, and he loved having sex. Cocaine and, later, freebase cocaine, was just another vice that Gonen suspected would eventually beat him. Gonen didn't mind—from the moment he first inhaled a thick cloud of cocaine smoke, Gonen loved freebasing.

He also loved Honey Tesman—so much by that point that he never did take her to the swingers' club. The thought of sharing her sickened Gonen.

'I was in love with her,' Gonen said. 'I couldn't bring her there and watch her fuck other guys.'

Gonen hired a prostitute to accompany him instead.

3

ADDICTION

JUST AS QUICKLY as he had fallen in love with Tesman, Gonen fell in love with freebase cocaine. That didn't sit well with Ran Ephraim, who had made good on his promise to move to New York City.

Honey Tesman's apartment at 32nd Street and Second Avenue in Manhattan was an open house party. An endless string of models, bodybuilders, corporate climbers, aspiring actors, and club kids crashed on her couch and kept the 32-year-old coke addict company as she stayed up late and held court in the crowded quarters.

Since Ron Gonen was paying her rent, Tesman let him use her apartment as a base of operations for his growing cocaine empire. He also kept an apartment on the eighth floor of the Chelsea Hotel, where two kilos and a scale were always tucked under a loose floorboard and where he could slip into El Quijote, the lobby restaurant, to meet clients. He had a third apartment, a 'clean' apartment with no drugs or paraphernalia, at 43rd Street and Third Avenue. He was snaking his way into every social group in Manhattan. On his own he had hooked the artists and writers he met through his friends at the Chelsea Hotel, and through Tesman, he was meeting the powerful people and Manhattan social climbers who craved cocaine.

But an apartment like Tesman's, an apartment where people were always around—her nosy, gay house cleaner, bodybuilders who wanted to sleep with her, would-be models—was a risky place to do business. Gonen had told Tesman she needed to tone down her entertaining, but as she did so often when asked to do something, Tesman shrugged and ignored him.

Ran Ephraim, who had been making frequent visits in preparation for his move to New York, added another layer of oddity to the nightly gatherings at Tesman's house. Ephraim's English was broken and his clothes were very un–New York. He still wore his hair in a buzz cut and preferred military issued cargo pants and paratrooper boots instead of the designer jeans and cashmere sweaters that Gonen wore. Usually Ephraim sat quietly in the corner, too timid to talk and too proud to take part in the binge drinking and casual drug use that surrounded him. He had been told he had the good looks of Robert Redford: chiselled features, perfect teeth, and an engaging smile. But he rarely smiled, and any tenderness in his look was usually offset by a scowl.

Gonen could never determine if Ephraim was really pissed off or just overwhelmed, as so many first-time New Yorkers are. As host and dealer, Gonen had little time to attend to his friend. During a party he would check on him every hour or so, speaking in Hebrew, but Ephraim seemed content to sit in the corner and watch the madness that unfolded before him. At the same time, Gonen saw Ephraim as a possible cure for the apartment's constant overcrowding syndrome.

They had been out to dinner, and then to a few jazz clubs Tesman favoured. Three girls who claimed they were models accepted invitations to go back to Tesman's. There were two bodybuilders waiting when they returned to the apartment, as well as a male model for cigarette billboards who slept on Tesman's sofa. Gonen could never remember which brand he he was the face of; Tesman just called him 'my Marlboro man.'

Ephraim was tired. For the past several months, he had had no social life, watching television in his Los Angeles motel room and occasionally going out for a solitary dinner. Going out night after night was exhausting, and he was visibly perturbed when Gonen said they would once again be crashing at Tesman's apartment. He was sick of fighting with the Marlboro man for the more comfortable of the two couches in Tesman's haphazard living room, sick of staying up until six in the morning, and sick of feeling like an outcast.

'Don't worry, we'll go to bed early tonight,' Gonen said during one of his hourly pep talks. 'I have a plan.'

Five minutes later, Gonen nodded to Ephraim. Gonen hadn't fully thought out his plan. He hadn't thought about how angry Tesman would be, or how Ephraim would terrify her guests. When Ephraim reached into the zipper pocket of his leather jacket, drew a 9-millimetre pistol, and started screaming for everyone to 'Get the fuck out'—just as Gonen had instructed—Gonen realised he might have selected a solution that was a bit too harsh for his relatively minor dilemma. This was a culture clash—two hardened Israelis and six upper middle-class kids who had probably never seen a gun before. And now one of the hardened Israelis was waving a gun around and threatening to shoot them all.

The Marlboro man was the first to sprint for the door. He tripped once, got up, and ran down the stairs two at a time. Tesman would never see him again. Several years later she heard that he had died of lung cancer. The models slowly gathered their purses and jackets from the couch with looks that screamed 'Whatever.' The weight lifters were first terrified and then angry—angry that the party was ending and angry that they weren't as tough as Ephraim's gun.

'That's fucked up,' one of them said as they walked out the door.

Honey Tesman pouted and scowled at Gonen and Ephraim. All three were silent for a few minutes after everyone left, and then the telephone rang. It was someone—Gonen wasn't sure who—looking to see if it would be OK to stop by.

'No, you can't come by tonight,' Tesman said, 'unless you want to get shot by Ron's crazy friend Ran.'

RON GONEN ASSUMED that Ran Ephraim wouldn't last in New York. He had been visiting a few times each month since announcing his plans to move to Manhattan, and with each visit, he looked more overwhelmed. Gonen assumed Ephraim would eventually decide to stay in Los Angeles, or find a way to operate his cocaine brokerage from Tel Aviv. At worst, Gonen thought, Ephraim would move to New York, spend a few months deciding he wasn't cut out for city life, and then move on.

What Gonen didn't know is that the day before Ephraim chased Tesman's friends out of her apartment at gunpoint, Ephraim had become a very rich man. And he owed all his wealth to New York City.

During each visit to New York, Ephraim made time to visit Raz and Luiz Ben-Zvi, a brother and sister in charge of the New York office of their family's gold business. Ephraim had met Raz in the Israeli Merchant Marine, which both joined after serving in the Six Day War in 1967. Gonen also knew Raz; in 1972, shortly after they met, Ephraim sent Gonen to Holon to pick up 1000 pairs of stolen Italian designer shoes from Ben-Zvi.

The Ben-Zvi family business was simple: Wholesale gold was purchased on credit, and then manufactured into gold chains and jewellery. When the jewellery was sold, the credit was paid off. The New York office, in Manhattan's Diamond District, was where Raz Ben-Zvi purchased gold to be shipped to the family's jewellery manufacturing plant in Israel.

It was a second-floor office and sparsely furnished, save for the safes that held the gold, as well as long tables and jeweller's scales. Though Ephraim and Ben-Zvi had not seen each other in several years, it only took the two old friends a couple of hours to come up with a sting to make them rich. With Ephraim's help, Ben-Zvi was going to rob himself.

On each subsequent trip, Ephraim would arrive with an empty suitcase and fill it with the heavy gold bars from the safe. Over the course of a few trips, Ephraim carted out more than $750,000 worth of gold, all of it purchased on Ben-Zvi's credit. Ephraim worked on selling it to the fences in Europe and the Middle East while Ben-Zvi continued to operate his business.

On the last trip, Ephraim tied up Raz and Luiz and ransacked the office to make it look as if it had been robbed that very afternoon. To make it look more convincing, Ephraim slugged Raz hard enough to leave a black eye.

'Why did you do that?' Ben-Zvi said, more perturbed than upset. He was seated next to his sister, their hands tied and feet bound.

'For the cops,' he said as he applied a strip of duct tape to each of their mouths.

A few hours later, worried when the brother and sister did not return to the apartment building where several relatives lived, friends and family members called the police. Ben-Zvi spent the next few days giving statements to the police and meeting with insurance adjusters. The insurance cheques were used to pay off the lines of credit he had opened with his gold brokers, and he and Ephraim split the cash proceeds from Ephraim's fencing activities. Ephraim had done well—each man walked away from the deal with more than $180,000.

Gonen suspected something had changed only after he started to help Ephraim get settled in New York.

Ephraim went from miser to spendthrift in a matter of days. He told Gonen to take him where he could buy furnishings for a new apartment, new clothes, and a second Rolex wristwatch. Gonen found Ephraim a sixth-story apartment in Tribeca and helped him fill it with expensive furniture, linens, and stereo equipment. Gonen, who loved to cook, found himself envious as he helped Ephraim pick out top-of-the-line cookware and kitchen gadgets.

Ephraim paid for everything in cash.

It didn't add up. Gonen knew that Ephraim had no other cocaine customers. Gonen was only buying one or two kilos a month from him, preferring Spencer's quality and prices. Ephraim, at best, was walking away with $7,000 profit on each deal. While $14,000 a month was considerable, it was not enough to sustain Ephraim's new lifestyle.

'I don't know how, or even why, you're buying all this stuff,' Gonen said. 'How long are you planning on staying?'

'For good,' Ephraim said. 'I like New York.'

'So what's going on?' Gonen asked as they left another art gallery looking for décor for the apartment and climbed into his car. 'Where is all this money coming from?'

Ephraim told him the story, starting with 'Remember my friend Raz Ben-Zvi?' And then the story came cascading out, the suitcases full of gold, the insurance checques, and the phoney statements to the cops. 'I even punched the motherfucker, gave him a black eye,' Ephraim said. His English was sketchy—everyone, in Ephraim's limited use of the language, was a motherfucker. Gonen was upset, not only because Ephraim would now be staying in New York and creating uncomfortable social and business situations, but because he hadn't been included in the score.

'Next time,' Ephraim said. 'Next time, I'll bring you along. And we'll get Raz to buy a lot more gold ahead of time, so it will make this one look like nothing. For now, we need to focus on cocaine.'

The 'we' made Gonen squirm. Ephraim explained he now had more than enough cash to front Gonen cocaine by the kilo. It was a bottomless line of credit extended to a man who was sinking into the depths of a freebase cocaine addiction. But just like Gonen hadn't known about Ephraim's grand larceny, Ephraim had no idea that he was now dealing with a junkie.

FREEBASING IS NOT a social activity.

The slang term refers to the chemical reaction that frees the base of the cocaine, creating a more potent form of the drug. Previously, freebasing required dangerous chemical procedures and included the use of ether, which often had tragic results. In 1980, comedian Richard Pryor famously set himself on fire while preparing a batch of the drug. Pryor lived, but other freebase cocaine addicts weren't as lucky.

That had changed by 1982, however, when a new way of preparing freebase started to gain popularity. The new method simply required the user to mix a bit of baking soda and water with the cocaine in a glass vial. The vial was gently heated with a small torch, and the freebase cocaine rocks would float to the top of the vial. Addicts usually skipped the last step—drying the rocks under heating lamps—and moved the rock directly to their glass-lined freebase cocaine pipes. The end result was cocaine that ignited at a lower temperature and involved much less waste than smoking pure cocaine. Any substance that is smoked, be it nicotine or cocaine, travels through the bloodstream to the brain in about nine seconds. Addicts say the difference between snorting and smoking cocaine is the difference between drinking vodka and injecting pure alcohol into your veins. Within a few years, the new method of making freebase cocaine would be refined for mass production and unleash the American crack epidemic. It would also give rise to Ron Gonen's brutal addiction.

As simple as it was to make freebase cocaine, it was not an inconspicuous process. When he went to nightclubs, Gonen could not use sinks in the men's restrooms to fill the vials he was using to cook his cocaine, so he resorted to hiding in the stalls and scooping water from the toilet. Once the rocks were ready, the burning cocaine smelled like burning fibreglass and would never be mistaken for a cigarette. Gonen either got knowing looks or dirty looks as he left a stall after smoking base.

Cocaine users feel euphoric and talkative. The need for sleep and food is erased. Users are mentally alert and particularly in tune with the sensations of sight, sound, and touch. Many users say it helps them perform physical and mental tasks more quickly. On the downside, however, it can trigger paranoia, irritability, and depression. Perhaps worst of all, the drug's effects last, on average, for twenty minutes. Most users cover the short-lived effects of cocaine by ingesting more and more cocaine over the course of a night.

Or in Gonen's case, over the course of the next two years.

The old Ron Gonen would have never accepted credit, from Ran Ephraim or anyone else. The pre-cocaine Ron Gonen would have continued to pay cash for coke from Spencer, Ephraim, and his new Miami connections. He would have continued to work the nightclubs and retail clients night in and night out. But the old Ron Gonen didn't have to support his and Tesman's $350-a-day habit on top of three apartments. The old Ron Gonen didn't have to worry about finding a club with a private VIP restroom to cook base. The old Ron Gonen got restless if he had to stay at home; the new Ron Gonen never wanted to leave Tesman's 32nd Street apartment.

Gonen started dealing wholesale. The profit margins were lower, and, because he was dealing in quantities measured in kilos as opposed to grams and ounces, the potential jail sentences were longer. The only real advantage to dealing wholesale was he only had to meet with a couple of clients each day, and those clients could be instructed to meet him at Tesman's apartment. Ron Gonen, who a little more than a year earlier had arrived in New York hoping to grow a cocaine business, was watching that prospect shrink in the clouds of freebase cocaine smoke emitting from the pipe he kept tucked in a boot wherever he went.

That only added to Ran Ephraim's anger management issues. Ephraim had only been selling a kilo or two a month from Los Angeles and had come to New York to work next to his only cocaine distributor and increase his take. And now that distributor was frequently absent from his usual hangouts and nearly impossible to track down by telephone. The only thing growing was the line of credit Ephraim had given to Gonen, first to $6,000, then to $10,000 and, by the end of Ephraim's first summer in New York, to $16,000. While waiting for Gonen to pay, he was burning through his six-figure bankroll—the same money he had hoped to use to set up other dealers and build his business.

Gonen, for his part, stopped answering the telephone, preferring to call back whoever left him messages. Ephraim was like a collection agency, calling at all hours of the day and night. Finally Gonen made arrangements to have a stolen painting by the famed 19th-century Impressionist artist William Turner transferred from London to New York. Gonen still had a key to Ephraim's apartment. Ephraim had started dating Gonen's Chelsea Hotel friend, Rita Fecher, and through Fecher, Gonen learned of a night when the couple would not be home. On that night—a night that Gonen knew Ephraim and Fecher were attending a gallery opening in hopes of bolstering Ephraim's front as an art dealer—Gonen moved the painting and two of his four 9-millimetre Benelli pistols with silencers to the apartment and arranged them on Ephraim's glass-topped coffee table. He left a note implying that the art and guns were collateral for future payments against his debt.

Ephraim and Fecher returned a few hours later. The painting and the pistols startled him—until he read the note. His face went crimson, and Fecher was immediately terrified as she watched Ephraim—who had been nothing short of charming until that very moment—melt down. 'A painting I can't sell and guns I don't need for $16,000?' he screamed. 'The motherfucking junkie!'

Ephraim found the phone and called the desk of the Chelsea Hotel. No, the man at the front desk said, no one had seen Gonen all week. He called Tesman's apartment and let the phone ring several times. When no one answered, he hung up and called the clean apartment, where Tesman picked up.

'Where is he?'

'He's not here,' Tesman said.

'You're lying to me,' Ephraim said. 'I just want to talk to him.'

'I haven't seen him all night,' Tesman said. Ephraim slammed the phone down so hard the plastic cradle cracked.

Without acknowledging Fecher, Ephraim stormed out of the apartment. But he didn't stop to grab one of the pistols from the coffee table. Gonen, after all, was still his friend.

WHEN RON GONEN returned to his 43rd Street apartment a few hours later, the first thing he noticed was that the door was slightly ajar and some of the wood along the door frame was splintered. Then he heard Tesman sobbing.

A chair was overturned and there were other signs of a struggle. Tesman was sprawled out on the couch, facedown and holding a bag of ice to her back. Both of them were high, and Gonen tried to calm her down and coax the story out of her by passing her his loaded freebase pipe. As best he could tell, Ephraim had shown up looking for him, and Tesman had tried to explain through the chained doorway that Gonen hadn't been there all night. Then Ephraim had tried to push his way through the door while Tesman—all of 110 pounds—tried to hold back Ephraim's 220-pound bulk. Finally he kicked the door open. Tesman had turned to move out of the way, but not fast enough— the doorknob caught her on the edge of her hip, leaving a red, baseball-sized welt.

Strangely enough, that may have been the moment Gonen knew he really loved Tesman. He knew he really loved Tesman because he knew he was going to kill Ephraim for hurting her.

Horror swept over Tesman's face as she watched Gonen check his two remaining pistols and silencers and slide one into each breast pocket of his blazer. He ignored her as he slammed the door of the apartment. Before he had even hit the landing in the stairwell, she was dialling Ephraim's apartment. She was mad at Ran Ephraim, but she didn't want to see him dead. Nor did she want to see Gonen shipped off to prison.

Rita Fecher answered the telephone. No, Ephraim was not there, he had left angry a few hours earlier and hadn't come home yet. Tesman tried to explain that

Gonen was high and threatening to kill Ephraim if he found him.

When Ephraim finally returned to the apartment, he seemed calm—at least for a moment, or at least until Fecher explained that Gonen had gone mad and left his apartment a few minutes earlier with two guns and a determination to kill Ephraim.

'This isn't worth it,' he said.

Ephraim started packing two suitcases and told Fecher she would have to go home. She needed to get out of the apartment before Gonen arrived—if he arrived. Fecher wanted to know where Ephraim was going. Ephraim said he wasn't sure. Completely packed, Ephraim took one last look at the William Turner painting. Gonen had bragged that the painting was his most prized possession. It was now a half-hearted effort to settle a debt. Ephraim went to a hallway closet and got a third suitcase for the painting, haphazardly throwing clothes around it and hoping airport screeners wouldn't pay too much attention to his bags when he went through customs.

On the street Ephraim hailed a cab and gave the driver directions to take Fecher to the Chelsea Hotel. Then he hailed another and told the driver to head toward the airport. His New York stint was over. Fuck the apartment, fuck the expensive furnishings, and fuck Fecher, for that matter. Ephraim was leaving New York and it would be more than a year before he would return.

SUICIDE AND THOUGHTS of suicide are textbook symptoms of cocaine withdrawal. Addicts partly attribute it to the overwhelming feelings of guilt that come the morning after a night of overindulgence. There are few options. An addict can just work through the depression and guilt. He can seek treatment. He can kill himself. Or he can find some cocaine. Gonen didn't think he was an addict and with loose kilos always nearby, he never had to look hard for another boost. The morning after he had threatened to find Ran Ephraim and gun him down, the first thing he did was cocaine.

Tesman seemed madder at him than she was at Ephraim and told him she wanted to sleep alone that night. 'You can't handle your high,' she hissed at him as she slammed the bedroom door. He had barely slept. Even when he calmed down enough to realise that he wasn't going to find Ephraim and, even if he did, he wasn't going to kill him, he had lain on his couch and stared at the ceiling.

He snorted a line of cocaine and lit a cigarette, hoping that would be enough to help him prepare a pot of coffee and a batch of freebase. As he staggered around the living room and kitchen in boxer shorts and a T-shirt, he tried to replay the previous evening's events in his mind. He had a ringing headache—another familiar morning-after symptom for addicts. He cringed at the spectacle he had made of himself and wondered what would have happened had he gone to Ephraim's apartment before looking for him at the gallery. The cocaine, Gonen hoped, would clear the headache, and he'd be able to figure out how much damage he had done.

He noticed the blinking red light on the answering machine as he exhaled his first hit of freebase. He didn't remember hearing the phone ring the previous night, but the call might have come when he was still roaming Manhattan or after he had come home to pass out. He played the message.

'It's Ran,' Ephraim said. It was obvious he was calling from a pay phone. 'I'm going to Tel Aviv. I'm not coming back.'

There were the familiar sounds of an airport in the background—the beeping of taxicab horns, the dull murmur of waiting passengers, and arriving flight announcements. He played the message a second time, then sat in the silence of the apartment. And that was it. For a moment—and only for a moment—Gonen was upset that they hadn't at least been able to talk that; he hadn't been able to apologise for slipping up. But then Gonen realised that with Ephraim gone, he had effectively cleared his $16,000 debt. And with his key to Ephraim's apartment, he now had access to all of his high-priced possessions.

4

'TIL DEATH DO US PART

It would be several months and countless mornings of waking up to a bloody pillow before Ron Gonen decided he needed to kick his cocaine habit. His solution was to leave a freebase-addicted girlfriend and move in with a heroin junkie.

Susan Cooper was an artist, poet, and party planner who lived in a luxury apartment in a tower near Washington Square Park. Her parents subsidised her lifestyle. On the day he decided to kick freebase, Gonen gave up his room at the Chelsea Hotel, changed the locks at his clean apartment uptown, and moved the few belongings he had at Tesman's place out. He had no plans to stop dealing cocaine—that thought never crossed his mind. His problem was that Tesman solved every dilemma by waving a freebase pipe in his face.

Cooper was 5 feet 7 inches tall and buxom, with long, dark hair and dark eyes. Gonen considered her 'a lousy lay,' but liked her enough to propose marriage during the three months he stayed with her. She was wary of marriage—she had only recently divorced her heroin-addicted husband and fled London, where they had been living and working as aspiring writers. Besides, Gonen was a gangster and that fact never settled well with Cooper. One of her pieces was a poem about being a gangster's wife, in which she wrote about crushing garlic with the butt of the gun and blackjack he kept in his suit jacket and slicing tomatoes with the double-edged knife Gonen kept in his boot. She made a collage to accompany the poem, which included photos of Gonen's gun, blackjack, and knife, as well as a photo which she had snapped—while he slept—of Gonen's penis.

'Is that my . . .' Gonen asked.

'Are those your weapons?' Cooper said. 'Yes, they are.'

Cooper's parents lived in West Orange, New Jersey, and on weekends she and Gonen would take the train out of Manhattan for Sunday dinner. Cooper's father was an electrical contractor and, not knowing that Gonen was a drug dealer, saw the handsome Israeli as a positive influence on his eccentric daughter. Things were stable for a while. His daughter had started working again and seemed to be cleaning up. Gonen was also cleaning up, and he assured her father, the diamond business—Gonen's front for his cocaine dealing—was undergoing unprecedented growth. Gonen was never tempted to join Cooper as she anxiously shot up heroin when they returned to the apartment. He had snorted the drug once back in Germany and had gotten ill.

Honey Tesman missed Gonen. It didn't take long for her to track him down. Within a few weeks, she was calling Cooper's apartment at odd hours. Sometimes she would just hang up. Other times she would ask to speak to Gonen, and when Cooper told Tesman he wasn't there, Tesman would call her a bitch. She showed up at the building but could not get past the well-dressed doormen. And then there was the bomb threat.

On a Sunday morning in early May 1984, Gonen and Cooper were thumbing through newspapers, killing time until they'd hop a train to Jersey. The knock at the door was unexpected, and both Cooper and Gonen were surprised to see the weekend doorman in the foyer of the apartment.

'There's been a bomb threat called to the building,' the doorman said.

'Oh my God,' Cooper said.

'We don't think there's an actual bomb,' the doorman explained. 'We think it's that woman—the one that's always calling for Mr Gonen.'

The doorman explained that Mr Gonen wasn't on the lease, and the building's management had no desire to add him to the lease. He also mentioned that it would probably be best for everyone if he ceased living in the building.

A few months earlier Gonen would have become enraged and scrambled into a back room to cook a batch of freebase. He would have loaded a pistol and left the apartment, vowing to end his Tesman problem once and for all. But not today. Gonen quietly began to gather his belongings.

'I understand,' was all Gonen said to the doorman.

And it was at that moment, in defiance of all reason, that Gonen decided the only way to keep Honey Tesman under control was to marry her.

RON GONEN AND Honey Tesman were married on 19 June 1984, in a city hall ceremony in New York. Gonen paid $20 for a witness, and he and the bride exchanged wedding bands that had been a gift from a jeweller who was also one of Gonen's customers. Immediately following the ceremony, Tesman pushed back through the line of couples waiting for their turn at wedded bliss and borrowed a city hall copying machine.

She mailed a copy of the marriage license to her mother in Oyster Bay, hoping the blood test would be proof enough to her family that she was off drugs.

Indeed, before he agreed to marry her, Gonen said that both he and Tesman would have to be sober. He set the ultimatum that there would be no more cocaine and they'd even try to live a normal life, outside of his ongoing narcotics distribution. He told her they would find a house on Long Island, which would keep her close to her family. He said he'd help her get permission from her family to start caring for her daughter once again. For several years her daughter had been staying with Tesman's sisters and her only real incentive to clean up was to once again live with her daughter. Gonen waited for three weeks before taking Tesman to city hall to make sure her sobriety would stick.

For her part, Tesman made a good faith effort to stop using cocaine. It was one of her better efforts— she was cocaine free for the three weeks leading up to the wedding and for a full week after the ceremony.

Gonen held out a bit longer. It would be late July before he was freebasing again.

'You've got to stop,' Rita Fecher told him one day when he was hiding from Tesman for a few hours at the Chelsea. 'Even if it means you stop dealing. Maybe you need to leave New York for a while.'

'Maybe if we had a kid ... ' Gonen said. He and Fecher were sitting in Fecher's Chelsea Hotel room. 'Are you nuts? You can't even take care of yourself!' Fecher said.

Fecher was still angry at Gonen for running Ran Ephraim out of the country. Only after Ephraim had called from Israel had she told Gonen that they had been seriously dating.

Gonen was off cocaine when she had told him. Before he stopped using, Fecher had feared Gonen's freebase-induced paranoia would have made him angry over their relationship. Now Fecher was angry. In addition to losing Ephraim, she had been undergoing treatment for colon cancer for almost as long as she had known Gonen.

'Do you know how hard it is to find someone who will fuck you when you have a bag of shit hanging off your side?' Fecher said, referring to her colostomy bag.

'You're just mad because your boyfriend couldn't be reasonable,' Gonen said.

'He couldn't be reasonable?' Fecher said. 'You're the one who's been high for two years.'

'I stopped for two months, and I can stop again,' Gonen said.

'You need to get away from it,' Fecher said. 'All of it. You're never going to stop using it as long as you're dealing it.'

Gonen didn't want to stop dealing cocaine, and if he wanted to celebrate his new wealth by snorting a few lines in the morning and freebasing his nights away, what business was it of Fecher's? He and Tesman were married, and they were, for the most part, happily married. They fought constantly, but it was the explosive personality that had attracted Gonen to her in the first place. Their makeup sex was intense, so intense that Gonen only occasionally felt the need to cheat on her.

Fecher was right in one respect. Quitting would be impossible as long as he was in New York. His whole life in New York had been cocaine. He tried to quit a few more times that summer, each time falling into a predictable pattern. On most attempts, he'd tell Tesman that he was leaving, that she hadn't kept her promise to keep off drugs and, in the process, had brought him back into addiction's fold. He would storm off, usually to visit an Israeli flight attendant he had met during one of her layovers.

Inevitably, Tesman would track him down or the draw of cocaine would grow stronger and Gonen would reconcile with her. As the summer wore on, as each new attempt at quitting failed, Gonen felt a growing desperation.

'IS SHE STILL there?' Tesman asked through the telephone.

She had tracked him down at the hotel where he had gone to hide with the blond flight attendant.

'No. She just left for the airport,' Gonen said.

'Do you want to come home?'

'Yes,' Gonen said.

'There's no blow here,' Tesman said.

'Meet me at Spencer's,' Gonen said. 'We'll pick up a couple of ounces, just for us and just to get us through the weekend. Then we'll both stop. Together.'

An hour later they were climbing into a cab in front of Spencer's loft, telling the driver to take them home. Gonen watched as Tesman tore into the cocaine—there was no shame, just an addict's greed and relief. She would never stop using, Gonen thought.

'Stop here,' Gonen told the driver.

Honey Tesman looked up from the cocaine, her face momentarily caught in the headlights of an oncoming car. Her pupils were fully dilated and there was a ring of cocaine around each nostril. 'What are you doing?' Tesman said.

'I need cigarettes.'

'Get me some.'

Gonen slipped into a corner store and bought a pack of Winstons. Then he turned and watched Tesman in the back of the cab. She had already resumed snorting coke, not even giving her heartbeat a few moments to settle down. If Gonen didn't get her home quickly, she very well might start cooking a batch of freebase right there in the back of the cab on the crowded street, where any cop might happen by. When she went down for another line, Gonen slipped out of the store and jogged a block over, where he hailed another cab.

He had the driver take him to a friend's apartment. An hour later, when his beeper started lighting up with calls from Tesman—no doubt they were angry calls—he threw it out the window and listened to it shatter on the sidewalk below the apartment.

The next morning, Gonen would wake up early and ride a cab to John F. Kennedy International Airport in Queens. He would pay cash for a one-way ticket on a flight to Israel that was departing that morning. Fecher had been right—he wouldn't quit until he got away from New York and away from Tesman. Like Ran Ephraim before him, Ron Gonen had been defeated by the chaos of New York.

RON GONEN ARRIVED in Tel Aviv in August of 1984, less than a week before his 36th birthday. He had no luggage, outside of the clothes he had been wearing for two straight days, and $7,500 in cash. He had spent the night before his flight at Avi's apartment, a close friend who was helping eye doctors revolutionise optical surgery with audiovisual equipment he was developing.

They played backgammon for most of the night. Gonen was going through the first few hours of cocaine withdrawal and was too jittery to sleep. But he still managed to smile like a man newly freed. He was talkative and explained his next move to Avi.

'I have to abandon everything and everybody,' Gonen said. 'I have no other choices.'

Since marrying Tesman earlier that summer, Gonen had been depressed and wracked with guilt. His cocaine business was barely enough to cover his lifestyle, although he conceded he would be better off financially if he didn't spend more than $10,000 a month on their habits. Because of Tesman, he was sullen and still addicted. By the time he boarded a flight to Tel Aviv with a one-way ticket, he couldn't have cared less if he ever saw her or New York City again.

He checked into the Hilton Tel Aviv. For the next five days, he hid in his room, living off of room service and only leaving to go downstairs to the hotel's steam room. The steam room felt cleansing. To Gonen, it felt like the hot water was driving out the poison he had been ingesting for the past two years. His ninth-floor room had a balcony overlooking the beach, and from there, he could see his old friends—the lifeguards who used to spend time in his bar and the gangsters who spent their days huddled on one end of the beach, talking through stings and deals and watching girls walk by. He even spotted his ex-wife, Doris Calle.

It had been over a year since they had spoken. Gonen had flown Calle to New York to arrange a quick divorce with a cheap attorney in Chinatown. Tesman had even thrown them a divorce party. They had split on good terms, but lately Gonen had avoided taking her phone calls; he had not sent her an alimony cheque in several months and knew she would be angry.

From his hotel room, he could see Calle's apartment—*their* apartment. In the morning he watched her leave with *his* dog, then stroll the length of the long beach, flirting with the lifeguards, tourists, and gangsters along the way. She was 43, but most people would have guessed she was not that far into her 30s. Gonen would watch her return late at night from whatever nightclub or café she had been to. He always felt relieved when she returned home alone.

Gonen dried out and felt the sharp pain of addiction wane. His cravings for coke were less intense after a few days, a minor annoyance instead of a full-blown obsession. Besides, he knew the crap he would buy in Tel Aviv wouldn't compare with the pure cocaine he had been doing in the United States. On his fifth day back in Tel Aviv, he felt well enough to go visit his mother in Holon. On the sixth day, he felt bold enough to call Doris Calle.

'You've been in Israel for a week and you haven't called me?' Calle said. 'Have you called anyone?'

'No. I was sick. I was addicted,' Gonen said. 'I really fucked up. I needed some time to get my head straight.'

'Where are you?' Calle said.

'Look out your window. I'm at the Hilton.'

'Why don't you come over?'

Calle was a professional shoplifter, and her apartment was lavishly decorated. Her clothing was always top of the line. Each season Doris Calle would make a trip through Europe's hot shopping cities and return home with as many as 150 new articles of clothing. Along the way she might pick up a new picture frame for the living room or a new tapestry for her bedroom. Gonen had always marvelled at her ability as a thief— there seemed to be nothing too big or awkward for Doris not only to steal, but also to bring back on an airplane.

Since the time they had moved from Germany to Israel in the late 1978, Gonen had never spent more than a few weeks at a time in the Tel Aviv apartment. Gonen greeted his dog as he and Calle got caught up. Calle had stopped seeing the guy who had threatened to turn Gonen in to police when he first started shuffling drugs between New York and Tel Aviv. Ran Ephraim was supposedly back in Tel Aviv, but Calle hadn't seen him. Life, Calle said, was simple but good. She could always use more money, but lately she had been selling some of the clothes she had been stealing in Milan and Paris for extra money. Gonen's life hadn't been so simple. Calle had seen him use cocaine when she went to America for their divorce, but she hadn't seen him at the height of his addiction. She didn't seem surprised that he had married Tesman, whom Calle said she genuinely liked.

'What are you going to do for money?'

'I don't know yet,' Gonen said. 'I'm spending $200 a night at the Hilton, so I need to come up with something fast.'

'Stay here,' Calle said. 'It will give you time to figure out something you can do for money, instead of doing something stupid, like dealing drugs.'

That night Gonen returned from the Hilton with the few clothes he had purchased during his week in Israel. When he went to put them in the spare bedroom, he could barely open the door. The room was crammed with racks of expensive dresses, boxes of shoes, and makeup tables heavy with jewellery. Calle, Gonen immediately knew, had been travelling a lot.

'That's my inventory,' she said. 'I'll end up selling most of it.'

'You need to open a store.'

Calle laughed.

'No,' Gonen said. 'I'm serious. You and I are going to open a boutique.'

GONEN WAS NEVER sure whether it was getting away from Tesman or his new project that fully cured his cocaine addiction. But he does know that any lingering cravings he had for cocaine were erased when he started working on 269, an upscale boutique in Tel Aviv's prime shopping and nightclub district. Gonen was manic about the idea. Within 36 hours of discovering Calle's clothing stash, he had leased a storefront, set up business bank accounts, and started painting the interior of the new store. He had lugged in display racks and moved everything from the spare bedroom to the storefront. Gonen took out advertisements in the newspapers and booked a trip for Calle to go to Milan to boost more merchandise.

By 14 September, the store was open from noon to midnight to lure in the passing nightclub kids. On opening night, Gonen stood in front of the boutique behind a long table, pouring cups of sangria and passing out beer and snacks to whoever happened by. There was an immediate vibe to the place, and within a week, 269 was taking in $3,000 a day. Because almost everything they sold was stolen, their expenses were minimal. Calle and Gonen were splitting 70% of the gross.

And then Honey Tesman called.

'Have you forgotten that you have a wife?'

Gonen stammered, unable to respond.

'Forget about it. It doesn't matter,' Tesman said. 'Just make sure you're at the airport at 8pm tomorrow to pick me up. If you won't stay with me in New York, I'm coming to Israel to stay with you.'

Gonen cringed. He loved Tesman, but he was also starting to love the idea of living straight. He had a mental image of her arriving in Tel Aviv with a suitcase full of blow, and the resumption of his addiction. He needed more *time*, time to continue thinking about things other than drugs, time to work out the last hunger pangs for cocaine.

'I can't be a junkie anymore,' Gonen said. 'You're poison.'

'I'm *clean*, Ron,' Tesman said. 'Just pick me up at the airport. You'll see.'

Tesman *was* clean and looked healthy when Gonen picked her up at the airport. She had gained some weight—she had been dreadfully thin when he abandoned her in the taxi cab—and her clothing was new and neat. Her eyes weren't nearly as glassy as they had been when he last saw her, and she was tanned. She said she had gone to her mother's house to clean up after he had left.

'You mean you went to visit your mother, and she wouldn't let you leave after you ran out of cocaine,' Gonen said.

'Does it matter?' Tesman said. 'The point is I'm clean now.'

Gonen drove Tesman to the boutique, where she greeted Calle with a hug. The last time they had seen each other was at the divorce party Tesman had thrown them at Casa Bella in Little Italy. Tesman, assuming everyone did as much cocaine as she did, had taken Calle to the ladies room and set her up with a line as thick as a pinky. Only after Calle had consumed several grams of blow, only after her heart started racing and she broke into a cold sweat, did Tesman realise Calle had never tried the drug.

'I thought everyone had done it,' Tesman said.

'I haven't,' Calle said. 'Am I going to die?'

It was a big enough scare that some people at the party speculated that Tesman was trying to kill Calle. Calle didn't sleep for three nights—including a nervous flight back to Tel Aviv. But now, in the boutique, it was as if she and Tesman were sisters.

'Is this your place?' Tesman said to Calle.

'It's ours,' Gonen said.

'Whose?'

'Us—you, me, Doris,' Gonen said. 'We own it.'

The anger Tesman had reserved for Gonen disappeared. Since she had met him she had known that behind the criminal swagger, he was a driven and intelligent man. And now she was seeing just how enterprising he could be. All he wanted—all she wanted—was to be happy by any means necessary. For the first time in their life together, and, really, for the first time ever in her adult life, things seemed normal to Tesman. She cried.

BUT FOR GONEN, crime always seemed like the easiest option. It was what he was good at. Tesman had talked to him about opening a franchise in her brother-in-law's chain of locksmith stores, or going back to school to become a realtor. But all that seemed like work to Gonen. He was even undeterred when, two weeks later, he met his criminal mentor in a café a few blocks away from the boutique and caught a glimpse of how his life could turn out.

Sammy Merkel had been a legend in Munich throughout the 1970s, the mastermind behind a series of high-profile burglaries that remain unsolved to this day. It had been nearly ten years since Gonen and Merkel had spoken. After leaving prison for a second time, Gonen had gone to London and over the course of eighteen months stole $4 million in an elaborate fraud ring. Merckel and other members of his German crew had always felt slighted that Gonen hadn't included them in the sting.

Merckel seemed to have forgotten about Gonen's time in London and was happy to see his protégé. Gonen, on the other hand, was saddened by the reunion. Merckel had moved to Tel Aviv permanently and had given up the criminal life. He was poor.

'You get too old for that shit,' Merckel said. 'You'll see—you'll hit 40 and you'll realise a ten or 15-year prison sentence might as well be a life sentence. You're doing the right thing with that little boutique of yours.'

The boutique wasn't exactly legal, but neither was it criminal enough to give Gonen the income and adrenaline rush he craved. It had been open for barely a month and already it was weighing on Gonen. It was the closest thing he had had to a job in the past 15 years, and he found himself spending nearly every waking hour there. What Gonen really wanted was his old life: a few jobs each year, and the rest of the time spent relaxing on the beach with his criminal buddies.

They talked for a while longer before Merckel said, 'I see your friend from New York came back.'

Gonen knew immediately that Merckel was referring to Ran Ephraim.

'Have you seen him yet?'

'No,' Gonen said.

'Well, you can,' Merckel said. 'I see him every day, sitting in that art gallery across the street.'

Ran Ephraim had bankrolled a gallery for Yosl Bergner, the famed Austrian-born Israeli painter. When Gonen entered the gallery, Ephraim was seated behind a desk, displaying as much pride and confidence as if he were the artist himself. He had ditched his military garb for an expensive suit. It was a beautiful gallery with wood floors and soft track lighting illuminating Bergner's work. Bergner's son-in-law managed the gallery and its day-to-day operations—Ephraim merely played a part.

People like Ephraim never went legit. In addition to selling counterfeit limited-edition prints of Bergner's work, he was laundering money for Raz Ben-Zvi and loan sharking.

Ephraim, who had been irate when Gonen tried to clear his debt with a stolen William Turner painting, hinted that he had gotten most of the money for his operation by selling that painting. Their debt cleared, Gonen didn't mention the scar on Tesman's back stemming from the night Ephraim had burst into her apartment.

Ephraim had also replaced Mickey, his ex-wife, and Rita Fecher, his New York girlfriend, with Judith Lustman. She was a Moroccan Jew and had been Ephraim's maid, but within two weeks of her working for him, he had fallen in love. Lustman was used to dating sailors, thugs, and other toughs and had been wooed by Ephraim's newly acquired sophisticated mannerisms. She liked the fact that he was ex-military, but also an art connoisseur who seemed to have an endless stash of money. Gonen explained his own situation, complete with details of his ex-wife working happily alongside his new wife in his boutique.

But there was one thing Gonen didn't tell Ephraim, because he wouldn't know for sure for several more weeks, when Tesman went to the doctor: Gonen was going to be a father.

'DRUGS WERE ONE chapter in my life,' Gonen told Tesman as her June 1985 delivery date neared. 'Now I want to focus on my talents.'

Gonen still had a bum ankle and felt he was getting too old to be a cat burglar. He needed something with low risk and high payoffs—no child of his, Gonen told Doris Calle, was going to grow up with a father off in prison. So he tried other lines of work. He smuggled rubies from Brazil to skirt Israel's high taxes on jewellery, but the payoff wasn't worth the effort. He needed to remain independent and do what he did best: steal. The London scam, Gonen knew, would have to be his model.

In 1979, Gonen had moved to London and set up an import/export company as a front for a complex fraud ring. Gonen bought expensive imported wines, golf clubs, designer clothes, and other luxury items on credit, then immediately resold them at cut rates to Greek gangsters and other underworld operatives throughout Europe and the Middle East. The scheme would eventually collapse. It didn't matter—when the creditors went to look for the man who owed them millions of dollars, they'd go looking for Levi Ezanko.

Levi Ezanko had an Israeli birth certificate and an Italian passport. He had a German driver's license and a listed phone number. What he didn't have was a pulse. Gonen had stolen the identity of a dead man and crafted a set of forged documents that were so realistic it would take Scotland Yard two trips to the expensive Fleet Street offices Gonen had rented to confront Mr Ezanko with the fact that he was deceased.

But by the time the second trip rolled around, the offices were empty, and Gonen was on his way to Guatemala, which didn't have an extradition treaty with Great Britain.

Gonen's mistake had been renting the offices on Fleet Street. The only reason British authorities had shown up at the office was that they were conducting security checks on everyone working on Fleet Street who would have front-row seats to the parade following Princess Diana's wedding to Prince Charles, which was scheduled for June 1981. After eighteen months, Gonen had netted more money than he had ever imagined from the sting, but it was just as quickly over because he—posing as Levi Ezanko—had been foolish enough to actually *use* the office.

This time, it would be different. Gonen flew to New York and set up a dummy office. He befriended an IBM sales rep who said he had never left the United States. Over drinks one night, Gonen convinced the man to pull a passport with Gonen's photo. In exchange for the passport, Gonen gave the man $5,000. 'If anyone ever asks you about it,' Gonen told him, 'say someone stole your identity. Then call me.'

Using the new identity, Gonen filed the proper paperwork to set up a new import-export company.

Gonen was frantic in forming the business. The baby was on its way, and, after the initial buzz had worn off, sales at 269 had dipped below $500 a day. He needed the tens of thousands of dollars he could earn each month from an elaborate fraud operation. But when he was just days away from placing his first order for merchandise that would never be paid for, an odd thing happened.

Someone ripped him off.

Gonen had parked his 1985 Volkswagen convertible near the Chelsea Hotel. He left the briefcase with all the paperwork for the business in the car. When he went to the car the following morning, the canvas roof had been slashed with a knife and the briefcase was gone.

It was a huge setback, but Gonen was determined to find a way to make a living without the temptations of addiction. At the same time, Tesman seemed determined to keep drugs front and centre in their lives.

They had just pulled off their latest sting— purchasing $30,000 in traveller's cheques, which

Tesman reported stolen at the same moment Gonen was cashing them in Amsterdam—when Tesman demanded a three-day trip to New York. She was seven months pregnant, and doctors in Tel Aviv had already scheduled a C-section for 19 June 1985, their first anniversary.

Gonen was wary of letting his wife go.

'What if I die during the C-section?' Tesman pleaded. 'I want to see my family in case something happens.'

Gonen relented. Keeping Tesman happy had become a priority. In the past three months, he had spent what little money they made from the boutique on moving his stepdaughter to Tel Aviv, which also involved careful negotiations with Tesman's ex-husband. He had rented a penthouse they could barely afford and had spent thousands of dollars on prenatal testing to monitor the unborn baby's health. After all that anguish, what was a trip to New York? Privately, he liked the idea of having Tesman away for a few days.

Gonen forgot all about his concerns until the day before Tesman was due to return to Tel Aviv, when two plainclothes Israeli police officers showed up at the door of the penthouse. They were members of what Gonen and his gangster pals called the Israeli 'secret police.' Their job was to collect information, and the information they had collected that afternoon was that Tesman had boarded a Tel Aviv–bound flight in New York with a kilo of cocaine.

Tesman hadn't gone to New York to see her mother. She had gone to New York to get high. Gonen found out that Tesman had spent three days in a hotel room ordering coke from a cab driver Gonen had once sold to. Only later would he find out that it was the cab driver who had called in the anonymous tip who would later confess he was getting back at Gonen for disappearing and leaving him without a steady cocaine supplier. But Gonen knew none of that as the two officers stood in his foyer with Gonen's dog jumping up and shedding onto their neatly pressed suits.

'Fuck her,' Gonen said.

'Excuse me?' the officer said.

'Fuck her,' Gonen said. 'She's the junkie and she has the coke. Not me.'

'You realise we can hold you for 48 hours without charging you, don't you?'

Gonen looked at Tesman's 16-year-old daughter, who was startled by the sudden intrusion on a Sunday afternoon.

Leaving her alone to deal with the trauma of a soon-to-be prosecuted mother wasn't the best course of action.

'Fine,' Gonen said. 'You can stay here. I won't leave, and you can stay to make sure I don't leave. In the morning, we'll all go to the airport and talk with Honey.'

The next morning, Tesman would greet Gonen with a hug before noticing the two well-dressed men flanking him. Her bags were seized. She was not carrying a kilogram, as the cab driver had said, but she did have 48 grams of cocaine in her suitcase. It was not an insignificant amount, but, at the same time, no one wanted prosecute a woman who was seven months pregnant.

Instead the two officers told Gonen he was now a police informant. Once a week he would be expected to take an early morning walk with his dog down to the beach where he would meet an agent posing as another dog walker. Gonen was expected to give him any information that might be useful in building cases against Israeli criminals.

'I'm trying to operate in New York, and he wants me to be a rat in Tel Aviv,' Gonen complained to Tesman.

It wasn't the meetings that bothered Gonen—he had an active imagination and had no problem making up stories about fictitious crimes. Sometimes he would take a crime he himself had committed a decade earlier in Germany, replacing names and places with their Israeli equivalents. Other times he would substitute heists he had read about in crime novels. He was soon an expert on giving just enough details to make the story seem legitimate, but not so many details that his friends from the beach would soon be questioned. The secret police officers he met with never seemed to catch on. But Gonen knew it was only a matter of time before they did some fact checking.

'There's a fuse under my ass in Tel Aviv,' Gonen said.

Gonen knew he could try to replace all the paperwork that had been stolen in New York. He could spend hours standing in line at government offices, days dealing with banks, and weeks waiting for a replacement passport. He even briefly contemplated putting a full-fledged effort behind 269 to see if he could make it a legitimate and profitable business. But ultimately he took what he thought was the easy way out.

'There's nothing left,' Gonen told Tesman a week before their daughter was to be delivered. 'There's nothing left but fucking drugs.'

5

DAILY DEALS

MARIEL GONEN WAS born on 19 June 1985, her parents' first wedding anniversary. She was healthy, but that didn't stop Gonen from running Mariel through a series of tests to make sure Tesman's prior rampant drug use and her cocaine relapse during the pregnancy hadn't caused brain damage or worse. The baby was fine.

Being a father terrified Gonen. He wanted Mariel to have a good life, a life he and her mother had never had, but that required lots of money. Facing huge setbacks in setting up his fraud operation and intense law enforcement pressure in Tel Aviv, the only way Gonen knew to make money fast was to start dealing cocaine in New York again.

'You're crazy,' Doris Calle said. They were cleaning out 269. The store had been a quick fad, hot one month and not generating enough money to cover the rent the next. When he announced his decision to spend three weeks a month in New York dealing coke, Gonen also said they would need to close the store.

'It's going to be different this time,' Gonen said. 'Last time I was dealing a kilo and up. This time I'm dealing under a kilo.'

'And I'm only going to do it long enough to make enough money to do something else,' he added. 'Maybe something legitimate.'

'This was almost legitimate,' Calle said, waving at the nearly empty boutique.

Gonen didn't want to stop dealing cocaine. Cocaine was power, and every day he was in New York, Gonen used that power. Each morning he met Russian and Israeli gangsters from Brooklyn at the 10th Street Baths and brokered deals. They treated him with respect. So did the Italian gangsters running coke from uptown construction sites where they controlled the trade unions. When Gonen stopped by a site with a fresh kilo, not only would they give him a paper bag of cash, but also they'd send him across the street to the temporary brothel they loaded with Jersey girls looking for construction workers' paycheques. He never had to pay at the brothel. He still sold to some of his better retail clients, mostly an odd collection of Tesman's friends, ranging from Mob hit men to Long Island housewives. And, with Ephraim gone, he was free to buy cocaine from whomever he wanted.

Gonen had cocaine stashes throughout the city. He had befriended an elderly Russian grandmother living in a public housing project in Brooklyn and had a safe installed in her apartment. Gonen knew from experience that a safe was not foolproof. To secure his Brooklyn stash, he carted a dozen 25-pound lead weights to the apartment and stacked them on the floor of the safe. Even with the lead bars, there was still room for several kilos of cocaine.

After a scare going through security at Miami International Airport, Gonen didn't like the idea of flying to Florida to pick up cocaine. Even with the lax airport security in 1984, six or seven pounds of coke was hard to slip by screeners in a carry-on bag. So he recruited the Russian grandmother.

Rhea doted on Gonen like a son, happy to have someone to speak Russian with. And when Gonen told her she could make an extra $500 a month just for taking a trip to Miami, she didn't hesitate. Gonen would fly down with her, show her how to tape the packets of cocaine to her body, and, when they arrived at the airport for their return flight, he would pretend he didn't know her. Once they had claimed their bags at LaGuardia, Gonen would drive her back to the project and leave a few kilos in the safe. And when the safe was empty, he didn't worry—he could always get more.

Cocaine was the easiest money he had ever made. As a cat burglar, he could spend weeks planning a job, only to have it scrapped when the vacationing jeweller came home a few days early. The drug culture was violent, but when a drug deal fell through, it didn't matter. There were always more deals that could be quickly brokered.

He wasn't smuggling drugs into the country, and with his stash spread throughout the city, he reasoned it was unlikely he'd ever get caught with enough to face serious jail time. His transactions were simple and could often be conducted with people he knew and trusted and in the privacy of his own home.

Getting back into cocaine after a year away, however, was not easy. Gonen's first visit was to Spencer, who had downsized from his luxury loft to a much smaller studio apartment. He was thin and jittery when Gonen visited him. It was clear that he, too, was now addicted to cocaine. He had nothing to sell.

'Everyone thought you were dead,' Spencer said. 'Now that you're back, everyone's going to think you're an informant.'

Gonen next tried Steve Rappaport. Rappaport would not have cocaine—he had been one of Gonen's best customers and the only person Gonen had ever met who consumed more of the drug than Tesman. Rappaport had worked as a writer for a small, hip advertising agency, where he had helped land major accounts. He had always liked keeping Gonen nearby—so much so that when the whole agency had to go to Miami to shoot a Jordache Jeans commercial in 1983, Rappaport had brought Gonen along.

'He's my consultant,' Rappaport had told the Jordache people who met them at the airport.

Rappaport was the quintessential 1980s New York man—well dressed, working until the late hours of the night, and partying until the early hours of the morning. He and a group of friends had formed the small agency and made more money than anyone knew what to do with.

So Gonen was surprised when he called the agency and found the number was disconnected. He tried Rappaport's apartment; that number was disconnected as well. He had Rappaport's mother's address in Brooklyn. If he had fallen on hard times, he might be living with her, or at the very least, she would know where Gonen could find him. She had always liked Gonen—Rappaport had introduced Gonen as a friend from the ad business, and she had immediately begun peppering him with questions about life in Israel.

That first afternoon back in New York, a yellow taxi cab dropped Gonen off on a rain-slicked Brooklyn sidewalk.

Rappaport's mother looked ragged when she answered the door. She hustled Gonen in out of the rain, and only when he was seated in the living room did he see the tears welling up in her eyes.

'You didn't hear, did you?' she said.

Gonen looked confused.

'Steve died two months ago.'

Mrs Rappaport told the story but Gonen didn't need to hear it—he could have guessed what had happened. A few weeks before he had left the United States, even in the throes of his own addiction, Gonen had known Rappaport was out of control. Gonen had cut him off, refusing to sell him any more cocaine. But it didn't matter. Rappaport had found a new dealer. He also found heroin.

He had been killed by a speedball, a potent combination of heroin and cocaine. The two drugs were combined in a solution and injected. Users were lower than rock bottom—they had even more dismal failure rates in drug treatment programmes than people who were addicted to one drug or the other.

Mrs Rappaport had suspected that her son was using drugs, but didn't think it was anything to worry about—he still worked long hours and he still made lots of money. If he said he was coming to visit, he would arrive on time and stay for hours. Only at the end—only when it was too late—did she see what a terrible drug problem her son had. Everyone he worked with was equally addicted, and it wasn't long before the agency had blown a few assignments and lost a few major clients—and the lease on their expensive Manhattan office space. Rappaport had also lost his apartment and had moved in with his mother in the weeks preceding his death, but he was rarely there.

'By that point, he was always out—always out looking for drugs,' Mrs Rappaport said. 'I thought about trying to find you, to see if you could talk to him. He always seemed to listen to you.'

Guilt crept into Gonen's stomach. The room suddenly felt small, yet Gonen wasn't quite sure how to explain to a widow who had lost her only son that he needed to leave.

'I think I need some air,' Gonen finally said.

Gonen rolled a cigarette and walked in a daze, looking for a taxi to take him back to Manhattan. Crime had always been a business, and, as a business, there was no place for emotion. It was quality that separated professional criminals from amateurs. In Germany, he had never worried about the violation his burglary victims would feel when they returned to find their homes ransacked. He hadn't worried about the midlevel London executive who may have lost his job for failing to do a thorough credit check on the import-export company that served as a front for Gonen's fraud ring.

But this was Steve—he had gotten drunk and stayed up all night with Steve. Steve had been at his divorce party. Gonen had promised to take Steve to Israel and show him his home land. They had talked about opening an art gallery together, something to fall back on when they burned out on their respective businesses.

'I felt guilty—more guilty than I ever had—about Steve's death,' Gonen would recall several years later. 'But there would be a lot more like him to feel guilty about.'

Gonen's guilt didn't last long. Within hours he had bought a kilo for $25,000 and was determined to undercut every retail dealer in New York. If the average dealer was selling cut grams of coke for $75, Gonen planned to sell pure grams for $45. Over the next few weeks, he would build a roster of steady retail clients and once again find himself pulling in cash, just as he had in 1982.

His clients were an eclectic mix of people. There was Jimmy, who managed a Coca-Cola bottling plant in Brooklyn and dealt cocaine on the side. There were two Jewish brothers who used to run all-night poker games above the Pizza Connection in Brooklyn. Rita Fecher started picking up nine ounces a month, and Reuben the Cuban was good for 18. Tesman's old boyfriend, Hank Appel, also bought nine ounces a month.

He started dealing from the 10th Street Baths as well. Michael Weatherby—a nine-ounce-a-week customer himself—introduced him to a high school teacher from New Hampshire. Once a month the teacher would drive down to New York and place $20,000 in a locker. Gonen would put half a kilo in a different locker, and, after a *shvitz*, they would exchange locker keys.

There was Roman Leningrad—Leningrad wasn't his last name, but the name of the city he had fled in Russia. He hung out at the 10th Street Baths, bought coke, and introduced Gonen to Alex, a Russian lounge singer who would buy four, five, or six kilos every two weeks to fly to Los Angeles. There was the fat Russian pimp who bought nine ounces a month. There was a famous Manhattan attorney who was good for nine ounces a week. There was an ordained minister, who became such a good customer that when he took a .22 calibre slug in the foot during an argument in Boston, he drove four hours straight to the Chelsea Hotel to ask Gonen for help. Gonen nursed the man back to health with a steady diet of cocaine and antibiotics.

There were connections in New Jersey as well. Leon started buying nine ounces a month, then introduced him to Hamilton Campos, a former Brazilian soccer star who was good for a half kilo every few weeks.

Cocaine did not discriminate and knew no class boundaries. When he looked through his address book after a few weeks back in New York, it was filled with people from all walks of life: plumbers and rabbis, fashion moguls and pimps, hit men and school teachers.

But there was something different this time around. Now that he was no longer using, he was profiting. In an average month, Gonen would net $40,000. He would spend three weeks in New York and a week in Tel Aviv, playing father and trying to keep his wife and ex-wife happy.

Supply lines were tight. Gonen had reopened his Miami connection, and also found a source in Los Angeles. He started using Rhea, the Russian grandmother who lived in the Brooklyn, as his mule. He even had a special girdle made for her to make it easier to load her up with a kilo of cocaine.

He would pay her between $500 and $2,500 for each trip, and even had wedding invitations printed that she could hand to customs officials when they started barraging her with questions in English, which she did not speak.

Vinny, Tesman's ex-boyfriend who had tried to poison Gonen, had come into possession of two kilos of cocaine stolen from New Jersey mobsters. The kilos were stolen by two young Italian kids who worked as dishwashers in Vinny's restaurant.

'They have more balls than brains,' Vinny told Gonen. 'I can't sell it—all three of us would get killed.'

The problem was the New York cocaine market was so tight that two kilos being sold to the wrong person could end in gunfire. Kilos of cocaine were stamped with logos that indicated where the cocaine came from and often its quality, almost as if they were brand names. 'Brands' that were in limited supply in New York—like the brand of cocaine the dishwashers had stolen—were noticeable. Vinny approached Gonen about selling them overseas.

Gonen called Bob, his silent partner in the London operation. Two days later Rhea was on a plane to London with the first kilo. Two weeks after that, she was flying back to London with a new wedding invitation to show to customs officials. Even after paying off Vinny and Rhea, Gonen walked away with $65,000 from each kilo sold overseas.

By the time the second London run was completed, Gonen had more than $100,000, in addition to the tens of thousands of dollars he was owed for cocaine he had copped to people on credit. He splurged and bought himself a 1973 Chevy Nova from a student on Long Island for $800. The car was beat up and ugly—the kind of car no one in their right mind would take the time to steal. Gonen spent another $4,000 outfitting it with a secret compartment behind the backseat where he could hide a briefcase stuffed with kilos of cocaine and his scale. He registered the car under a phoney name—the New York City police had just started a programme whereby any car that was towed off city streets would be checked by drug sniffing dogs. Dealers who weren't wise to the policy would be arrested when they went to claim their cars. Those who were smart enough to write off the car but still ignorant enough to register the car in their own names would have warrants issued against them.

JUGGLING HIS TEL AVIV trips had grown increasingly difficult. Gonen never wanted to let his New York clients know he was gone for a week every month, fearing they might find a more New York–centric dealer. So he worked up elaborate lies, telling clients he was in Miami, or Los Angeles, or that a shipment had gotten delayed and he'd need another day. He'd set up meetings in New York that he had no intention of attending, then wake up in the middle of the night in Tel Aviv to call the person and cancel. He started working out of the art gallery Ran Ephraim was operating, smoking cigarettes and sipping coffee in between calls to his string of New York junkies.

'So let me get this straight,' Ephraim said. 'You live in Tel Aviv and you deal in New York?'

'Something like that,' Gonen said.

Gonen downplayed how much cocaine he was dealing when he spoke with Ephraim. He could see Ephraim thinking about their previous foray into the New York City cocaine market. Ephraim started hinting that now that Gonen was sober, it actually might work.

'I'm not really dealing cocaine. Just a little—a couple of grams here and there,' Gonen said.

'You seem to be spending a lot of time there if you're only dealing grams.'

Gonen told him he was mostly dealing diamonds. When the boutique folded, he had needed a way to make a lot of money in a short amount of time. He said that he had a mistress in New York and had found good places to gamble. New York, Gonen said, was fun. It gave him a break from Tesman and a chance to earn money without the Israeli secret police asking him a lot of questions. Ephraim didn't completely buy into Gonen's story, but he didn't press him to rejuvenate their partnership, either.

At least not yet.

'Well, if you change your mind about cocaine . . .'

'I won't,' Gonen said.

In March 1986, Gonen was in New York when Tesman called and offered him some relief from Ephraim's growing curiosity.

'I want to come home,' Tesman said. 'To New York. I can't stand raising Mariel away from my family.'

'Then come home,' Gonen said. 'Pack up all the shit you want to bring and leave the rest with Doris.'

'You're not mad?'

'No,' Gonen said. 'Thank God. Now I don't need to go back to Israel and see Ran Ephraim.'

IN APRIL 1986, Ron Gonen, his wife Honey Tesman, and their daughter Mariel became suburbanites.

When they decided to get married, Gonen had promised Tesman a house on Long Island that would allow her to be close to her sisters and her mother. But those promises had disappeared as quickly as their shared sobriety—within a week of their wedding, Tesman was using again, and Gonen started freebasing not long after that.

Now, barring Tesman's trip to New York when she was seven months pregnant, both she and Gonen had been straight for nearly two years. Gonen found an English Tudor–style house in Long Beach, a block away from the ocean and complete with a two-car garage, a contemporary kitchen, and three bedrooms. It rented for $2,500 a month—about a quarter of what he and Tesman used to spend on cocaine in a given month. It was expensive by 1986 standards but nothing for Gonen, who was once again the distributor of choice for coke addicts and small-time dealers in Manhattan. They had no furniture, so Gonen spent three days outfitting the house with top-of-the-line bedroom sets, living room arrangements, and kitchenware. By May, the house was ready for Tesman, Mariel, and his stepdaughter to move into.

Gonen dumped the Chevy Nova to better fit in with his new, upper-middle-class neighbours. By all outward appearances, the Gonens were 'normal.' They made arrangements for his mother—still oblivious to her son's true profession—to come from Tel Aviv to visit for the summer. On weekends they would go to one of Honey's sister's houses for Sunday dinner. On Monday morning Gonen would wave to his new neighbours as they waited for buses and trains or warmed up their cars, all of them heading to Manhattan for another day of work. Gonen told his new neighbours he worked in the Diamond District, which was at least partially true: Some of his best cocaine customers were jewellers in the District. They would even loan him samples—diamonds, expensive tennis bracelets, and other jewellery—to keep in his briefcase in case one of his neighbours said he was in the market for a gift for his wife or daughter.

Gonen had three beepers: one for customers who bought a kilo, one for customers who bought less than a kilo, and one for Tesman. He was the first person he knew to own a portable phone, and he routinely ran up $1,200 monthly bills.

The normal life didn't last for long.

To Tesman, New York smelled like cocaine. It wasn't long before she was dropping hints and asking

Gonen who he would be dealing with on a given day. She'd ask about the quality of the product and joke that she should sample it—she always had a better nose for quality than he did. When that didn't work, she asked him bluntly for cocaine. And when he still refused, she would find kilos he had hidden around the house, breaking into the plastic and taking whatever she needed. She didn't see any reason to reseal the kilos and pretend like she hadn't been diving into his stash.

'I never felt there was anything wrong with drugs,' Tesman said. 'I was never ashamed, and I never felt guilty.'

They never formally separated, but Gonen did feel enough pressure to take a second apartment. It was a beautiful, fourth-storey walk-up at 80th Street and Columbus Avenue overlooking the American Museum of Natural History and Central Park.

For his part, Gonen was never tempted to fall back into addiction. In Israel, he had started a daily routine of running on the beach, and he continued to exercise once they returned to New York. Gonen focused on a different addiction: money. His cocaine business continued to grow, and he continued to map out new scores, new supply routes, and new clients in ways he never would have been able to if he didn't have a clear head.

By autumn they had fallen into a predictable routine. On weekends they would act like a family at the Long Beach House. They spent holidays with Tesman's sisters, pretending that addiction was a dark family secret tucked safely in the past. Tesman would talk about Mariel's play dates, and Gonen would brag to his brother-in-law about how well the diamond business was turning around.

Gonen would spend Monday through Friday at the apartment in the city, dealing. He started most days at the 10th Street Baths, then returned to the apartment for a few hours, waiting for the junkies to wake up and start pinging his beepers with frantic messages. On days when Tesman was particularly out of control, Gonen would bring Mariel into the city with him. He soon found that having a baby in the car seat next to him had its advantages—on the few occasions he was pulled over, the cop didn't linger long over his expertly forged documents or stop to consider that there might be $50,000 worth of cocaine tucked into a custom-built compartment in the car door.

The one person who could upend this routine, Gonen thought, was safely back in Israel, scamming wannabe art collectors and laundering money. So when Ran Ephraim called in late October 1986, Gonen was firm.

'I'm just coming to give it another shot,' Ephraim said. 'I'll do my thing, you do your thing.'

Ephraim said that Judith Lustman, the Moroccan housekeeper he had molded into his girlfriend, had not been to America. He wanted to bring her there to get married. He had invested $250,000 into Raz Ben-Zvi's Josi Jewellery, a sum that would give him a steady income of $2,000 to $3,000 a month.

'And if that isn't enough, well, we'll rob the motherfucker again,' Ephraim laughed.

Ephraim's first stint in New York had been taxing on both of them. Ephraim had hated everything about the city, all the little quirks that had helped New York churn away so many people who had come there looking for their fortune. The canyon walls of skyscrapers made Ephraim claustrophobic; he always insisted that they drive to wherever they needed to be, even if they were only going a few blocks. He lived in a luxury building but felt his apartment was too small, and resented the doorman who smiled every time he left or returned to the building. Socially, he had never fit in, choosing to sulk at every party, nightclub, or dinner Gonen dragged him to.

'I feel like a maggot in this city,' Ephraim had complained a few weeks before Gonen gave him an excuse to leave.

But now he had renewed confidence. Gonen suspected there was something more in his decision to return to New York. He knew Ephraim could collect on his Josi Jewellery investment in Israel just as easily as he could arrange a wedding with Lustman in Tel Aviv.

'I'm not asking you to be my partner. I'm asking you to be my friend,' Ephraim said. 'Be my friend and help me get set up, just like you did the last time.'

6

THE CRAZY

HE WAS AN Israeli, so by default, he was an outsider in Manhattan. But Moussan Alyian had become a player in the underworld. He was a silent partner in Nirvana, a Times Square Nightclub, and he was a heroin supplier to some of the city's most notorious criminals.

One of his better customers was Tommy 'Karate' Pitera, the Bonano family hit man who supplemented his income by dealing drugs between contract killings. Alyian supplied the heroin that caused Pitera's wife to die of an overdose in 1987, but Pitera took it out on the female addict who had pressured his wife to try the drug. Pitera killed the woman and dismembered her body, dumping the remains in the Staten Island lot where he disposed of all his victims.

Alyian didn't worry about Pitera—they were friends and he knew that Pitera understood the consequences of the drug game. And he knew Pitera needed his heroin to maintain the drug trade he and gangster Frank Gangi ran out of their Just Us Lounge in Manhattan. In addition to being the heroin supplier of choice to Italian Mafioso, Alyian made a comfortable living running a string of insurance fraud operations.

On the evening of 2 January 1988, Alyian hosted friends at his apartment. At 1am, after his friends had left, he went to the Nirvana Club. He finished most nights there, and, on that night, he quietly sipped two Bloody Marys at a table in a relatively quiet corner of the club. Business was slow that night, Alyian remarked to a new cocktail waitress, noting that things always slowed down after the holiday season came to a close.

He left the club between 3am and 4am and drove a short distance to his brownstone apartment. He climbed the stoop but had trouble getting his key into the lock. Police would later determine that the cylinder had been stuffed with matches to stall his entry into the building.

While struggling with the lock, Alyian was shot three times. He rolled down the stoop and crawled to the middle of the deserted Manhattan street. His attacker beat him, unleashing a flurry of kicks and swings with the .357 Magnum he had used to shoot Alyian. The attacker delivered a final, fatal shot to Alyian's head, then jumped into a waiting getaway car.

At 5am, an anonymous caller reported a body was lying in the middle of his street. When police caught up with Frank Gangi, he denied knowing Tommy Pitera and said—truthfully—he had no idea who had killed Alyian or why he had been killed. When police went to Pitera's apartment, he angrily asked, 'Who gave you my address?' before noting that Alyian and Gangi had also been friends. The detectives told Pitera that Gangi had denied knowing him.

'What am I, a suspect?' Pitera said, before slamming the door. 'If you have anything else to ask me, talk to my lawyer.'

The trail had gone cold. It would be too late before police figured out that Johnny Attias, an Israeli who had been working in New York since the previous year, was Alyian's heroin supplier. They would never make the connection that a few weeks earlier, Attias, using an alias, had been arrested near Alyian's apartment for possession of a .357 Magnum—similar to the one used in the killing. When the case went cold, the best piece of information detectives had to work with came from an unnamed source who said he had seen 'a short man from Israel with green eyes' near Alyian's apartment shortly before the shooting.

A 1987 FBI report estimated that there were 2,500 suspected Israeli criminals in the United States. None of them was as bloodthirsty as Johnny Attias. Friends and associates were never certain why Attias killed Moussan Alyian, but Attias rarely explained his reasons for killing. It is possible but unlikely that Pitera had hired him—most believe Pitera would have killed Alyian himself if he wanted him dead. There were rumours that Alyian had made a pass at Attias' wife, Ofra, and there was speculation that Attias felt Alyian was taking too long to pay him for the heroin he was supplying. Another theory was that Attias wanted to take over Alyian's fraud business, which hinged on staging phoney robberies to bilk insurers. Attias didn't even tell Yoav Sinah, who drove his getaway car, why he killed Alyian.

Not even Ofra Attias knew the motive for the killing. It was, after all, Alyian who had helped them move to the United States. Alyian had rented them their first apartment in Manhattan after the couple arrived in New York. Shortly after the murder, they moved to Queens.

'The reason behind the murder was a dispute on the subject of drugs,' was the best Ofra Attias could offer investigators when she was arrested nearly two years later. The only fact that was clear was that Johnny Attias didn't need a reason to kill. He enjoyed it, and, more important, he enjoyed the power that came from running his fast-growing Israeli Mafia with force. While it would take the police a little while longer to understand just how deadly a crew Attias was running, by 1988 Attias had laid the groundwork to become the biggest heroin importer into the greater New York City area and planned to break into new rackets, including cocaine trafficking, fraud, contract killing, and loan sharking.

Before arriving in New York, Johnny Attias had spent most of his life in and out of prison. He had met Ron Gonen in prison when he was just 16 and Gonen was 18. He first met Ran Ephraim in prison, then again when he learned that Ephraim lived near his mother-in-law in Israel. Ephraim would later describe Attias to Gonen, and they would chuckle about their mutual friend. Ephraim said Attias had earned the nickname 'The Crazy' in the Israeli jail where Ephraim was being held on charges of selling counterfeit currency. He was the inmate who spent more time in solitary confinement than any other prisoner. As soon as he was released from solitary, he would attack another inmate or a guard and be sent right back for another multi-week stretch.

Johnny Attias met Ofra in 1978. She was just 20 years old and had just broken off with a live-in boyfriend she had been seeing for four years, with whom she had a child. Johnny wasn't put off that Ofra had a daughter. She was an attractive woman with blonde hair and big blue eyes who didn't seem to be bothered by the fact that he was a criminal. Years later, when she was arrested, one of the prosecutors who worked out a deal for her co-operation would concede that Ofra was beautiful but could not get past an overwhelming feeling that she was dealing with a woman who had been regularly abused by her husband.

The couple had their first child, Sandy, in 1979, but soon after their daughter was born, Attias got word that Israeli authorities were going to activate a suspended sentence against him. He fled to Germany.

After he left Germany, Attias reunited with Ofra and their daughter in England. For the next several years the couple bounced around Europe and the Middle East, separately and apart. After six months in England, Attias headed to France. He had heard a rumour that an Israeli living there could get him a phoney Moroccan passport that would make it easier for him to travel to and from Israel.

France, Ofra would later state, was where Attias learned how to deal drugs. The former pimp and petty criminal began dealing in kilo weights of heroin. Attias was arrested in France and extradited to Switzerland as a suspect in a murder case; after several months he was released for lack of evidence. It is not clear if Attias had committed the murder in Switzerland, but it is clear that he was capable of killing.

Attias was deported to Israel. He spent just one week there before returning to France, where it would only be another week before he was arrested for weapons possession and sentenced to a year in prison. Attias was released, but a few months later both he and Ofra were arrested after French police raided their apartment and found drugs, cash, and weapons. Ofra served a year in prison and returned to Israel to wait for Attias to finish his four-year sentence.

DURING THE YEARS that Ron Gonen was making secretive trips from Tel Aviv to New York, Ephraim started making secretive trips of his own. Ephraim was accompanying Ofra to France to visit Attias in prison and may have even had an apartment there, where he fell in with other Israeli underworld figures. Ephraim, who was friendly with Ofra's mother and knew Attias from their short prison stint together in Israel, paid for Ofra's plane tickets and travel expenses so she could visit Attias in the French prison. While visiting Ephraim in France, Ofra met some of the other men who would eventually move their entire criminal enterprise to New York City and become the core of New York's Israeli Mafia.

Ofra met Israel Mizrachi, who had dark, curly hair and a massive build and went by the name of Israel Alice; Albert Soussan, 'the Moroccan' or Beber, who promised Attias that he would help him get the Moroccan passport as soon as he was released; and

Amren Effasy, Beber's partner who would later help the Israeli Mafia open up heroin trafficking routes from Southeast Asia to the United States. Ofra also met Moussan Alyian for the first time.

By the time Attias was released from prison in 1987, Ran Ephraim had been living and working as a drug dealer in the United States for long stretches during the previous six years. Attias was furious when he travelled to Morocco to get a passport on Beber's insistence, only to have to return to France without the document. He was even angrier when he heard that Beber had been arrested and questioned about his phoney passport operation. He was paranoid that Beber may have told authorities about his own attempts to get a forged passport. After killing two men during a drug deal that didn't work out, Attias decided he could no longer wait for Beber to deliver the passport. Attias was confident that Ephraim's claims of America being a land of opportunity were true, and he moved to New York City in the summer of 1987. Ofra followed him there that fall.

'MY FRIEND, THE Crazy? Remember him?' Ran Ephraim said to Ron Gonen one afternoon. They were in Gonen's Upper West Side apartment.

'He's here—in New York,' Ephraim said excitedly. 'He's working in Brooklyn and Queens.'

Ephraim had arrived in New York for a second time, and he and his bride-to-be had been staying in Raz Ben-Zvi's crowded Queens apartment. Ephraim had stopped by to ask for Gonen's help finding an apartment and a hotel room 'for business.' He boasted that he was going to become a successful art dealer. His specific requests for a hotel room—within walking distance of 48th Street, 'not a shit hole but not too classy'—baffled Gonen. But it hadn't baffled him nearly as much as the news that Attias had been in New York for more than a year.

'Johnny?' Gonen said. 'He's not in New York. He's in Paris.'

There had been a dispute over a heroin deal in Paris, Ephraim said. Attias had arranged a sit-down to work it out, but Attias wasn't very good at working things out. He had shot and killed two men and wounded a third, then fled Paris and the double-murder charges using his brother's passport. Now in New York, Attias had a crew and was importing heroin from Amsterdam and Thailand by the kilo. He had already cornered most of the heroin market in Brooklyn and Queens and was eyeing Manhattan.

Once he had arrived in Queens, Attias had befriended another criminal named Eitan Haya, who had also recently arrived in the United States. Haya was born on 17 December 1952, the third of four siblings in a working-class Israeli family. Between 1969 and 1971, Haya was arrested ten times in Israel, the last arrest on murder charges. On 26 July 1971, he was sentenced to life in prison, but ten years later the sentence was abandoned by presidential order. He was the kind of person Attias liked: one with no qualms about breaking the law. Together, Haya, Attias, and 'Israel Alice' Mizrachi (who had followed Attias to New York) smuggled three tons of hashish from Turkey to New York. The hashish deal made the trio very wealthy. Haya alone had walked away from the deal with $4 million, and Attias' and Israel Alice's cuts were rumoured to be around the same figure. They had turned the profits from that deal into a plan to take over Brooklyn and Queens. They were flooding the outer boroughs with heroin and, along the way, loan sharking and setting up more traditional rackets. Gonen was able to put Attias out of his mind for the moment. He had Ephraim to deal with. He found Ephraim a hotel, the San Carlos on East 50th Street between Third and Lexington Avenues. It wasn't lost on Gonen that the hotel put Ephraim just three blocks away from Raz Ben-Zvi's Diamond District office, which was on 48th Street between Fifth Avenue and Lexington. Ephraim also requested a corner room that allowed him to keep track of who was coming and going on both 50th Street and Third Avenue.

At Ephraim's urging, Gonen also tracked down a 'black phone.' In the early 1980s, just as drug dealers started to use pagers, the telephone companies started blocking incoming phone calls to most pay phones. And every good drug dealer knew that the phones that did accept incoming phone calls were probably bugged.

The black phones sold for $800 and allowed the dealer to receive incoming calls wherever he could plug the phone into a phone jack. The phone had been developed by an Israeli electronics expert living in Brooklyn and could be used to hijack phone lines and place long-distance and overseas calls without charge.

'Just don't get caught with this,' Gonen said on the afternoon he dropped the black phone off at Ephraim's room at the San Carlos. 'It's major fraud and definite jail time if you do. You'd be better off getting caught with silencers.'

Ephraim rarely left the room, and it wasn't long before Gonen realised he was doing more than dealing art. The phone allowed him to arrange trans-Atlantic drug deals. Within a few weeks, Ephraim was co-ordinating deals involving anonymous couriers who brought as many as six kilos of heroin per trip, all concealed neatly in phoney compartments built into the backs of black Samsonite suitcases.

He was also dropping hints that he was strengthening ties with Attias, who was heading a crew of a dozen Israeli expats. The violent methods of the emerging Israeli crew didn't sit well with Gonen, but he still helped Ephraim.

'I'm happy to help him,' he told Honey Tesman. 'If I help him, I don't have to work with him.'

On one afternoon Ephraim and Gonen took the elevator from the room to the lobby of the San Carlos. Waiting for them were three dark-skinned men, all wearing expensive warm-up suits—similar to the ones favoured by the Italian gangsters working in Brooklyn and Queens. To Gonen, the three men looked ridiculous. But Ephraim smiled and greeted each with a hug.

'Hey, Baldy,' the short, muscular one said to Gonen after a moment. 'You don't say hello?'

It was Attias. He had aged well and was no longer the skinny punk Gonen had met 18 years earlier. He wore expensive jewellery and had neatly styled hair—

which in a way, Gonen thought, made the warm-up suit look even more ludicrous.

The other two men were silent; it was clear that Attias was the alpha male of the group. He and Gonen quickly fell into a conversation about cars, drugs, and about their time in an Israeli jail.

'We were just kids,' Gonen told the other three men as Attias laughed. 'We spent the whole time watching our backs so we wouldn't get raped.'

Accompanying Attias were Eitan Haya and Israel Alice. Haya was known for being an ugly man with an incredibly attractive wife—a wife, incidentally, that Attias was rumoured to be sleeping with. He was short—Gonen says Haya looked like 'a miniature, shaved, Osama bin Laden'—but he had a big personality. On weekends, he tore up and down Long Island on custom-built Harley Davidson motorcycles. In addition to his warm-up suit, Haya wore cowboy boots to add some lift to his 5 feet 2 inch build. Israel Alice was slightly taller than Haya. He was a quiet, imposing figure with dark eyes.

Attias invited Gonen out to his car to smoke marijuana. Gonen inspected Johnny's stash, which he immediately dismissed as 'white trash shit.' He knew it couldn't have cost Attias much more than $100 an ounce. He offered up a joint from his own supply, which cost him as much as $500 an ounce, plus a trip to Vermont to buy it direct from the grower.

'You need to get me some of this,' Attias said.

'Take this,' Gonen said, handing Attias what was left of the ounce of pot in a small plastic baggie.

'Talk to Ephraim about whatever I owe you,' Attias said. But Gonen knew Ephraim wouldn't have the $400 he was owed. It was Attias' way of establishing dominance over Gonen. It was his way of saying that when he wanted something, Gonen would make sure he got it and not worry about compensation. The next time Attias asked Gonen about getting him some marijuana, Gonen lied and said his Vermont connection had gotten busted.

'Even then,' Gonen recalled, 'I knew you didn't say 'no' to Johnny.'

7

MURDER BY NUMBERS

FOR JOHNNY ATTIAS, America was the land of the free ride. Attias was a common street thug who spent a good chunk of the 1970s and most of the early 1980s in and out of prison. He had served jail time in at least three countries—Israel, France, and Switzerland. In prison he had earned the nickname 'The Crazy' for his violent temper, but outside of prison, he was just a pimp and a lowlife. That is, until he came to America and became the kingpin of one of the most lucrative drug smuggling operations in New York City.

In New York, Attias commanded a new brand of respect that he hadn't secured in Europe and the Middle East. And despite his violent temper, Attias was charming. He made people around him laugh, and while he was in New York, he had a string of attractive girlfriends, many of whom were more than a decade younger than him, and none of whom seemed to mind that he was married.

'He could smile and joke with you one night and make you think you were his best friend,' Gonen recalled. 'And then the next morning he could be telling people he was going to kill you.'

After killing Alyian, Attias decided he was angry with Albert 'Beber' Soussan, who had tried to help him obtain his phoney Moroccan passport. Attias claimed Soussan was a snitch co-operating with authorities in Morocco to bring charges against Attias in the phoney passport scam. Asked why he was so concerned about relatively minor charges in a country he had no intention of going back to, Attias conceded to Eitan Haya that he also believed Soussan was holding a couple of kilos of heroin that he wanted to steal.

On 2 April 1988, Soussan was heading to John F. Kennedy Airport on Long Island to fly to Israel for an extended visit. After he had parked his car in the long-term parking lot, a blue car—loaded with Attias and his henchmen—pulled up behind him. Attias told Soussan to get his bags and get in the car. In addition to Attias—whom Soussan had been avoiding for several weeks—the car held Israel Alice, Eitan Haya, and Yoav Sinah, a 32-year-old deadbeat who provided some backup muscle.

Ofra Attias would later recall that Israel Mizrachi and Eitan Haya had arrived at Attias' house earlier that day. They were excited, and she overheard Haya saying that Soussan was in New York but would be heading to Israel. Attias, Ofra said, had befriended Haya soon after they moved to Queens, in large part because he had told Attias he knew Soussan's partner, Arman Effassy. Attias and Haya had even hidden in the bushes near where Effassy and Soussan were rumoured to be staying.

Left: Ron as a boy in the USSR, 1954.

Right: Bar Mitzvah photo, 1961.

Left: 17-year-old Ron and a girlfriend on his first stolen Vespa in Tel Aviv, 1965.

Above: Ron Gonen and Doris Calle celebrating Gonen's 22nd birthday on 31 August 1970, at the Tilbori Nightclub in Munich.

Right: Ron Gonen at a Munich nightclub, 1970 or 1971.

Left: Ron and Doris in Ibiza, Spain in February 1971, celebrating a just-completed score in Munich.

Above: Doris, in the early 1970s.

Left: Honey Tesman and an unidentified friend use cocaine in New York City, 1982.

Right: Ron in Tel Aviv after his first big score, prior to going to Germany, 1970.

Above: The Tel Aviv boutique Ron Gonen and Doris Calle opened in 1984 where they sold the clothing and merchandise Doris had shoplifted.

Below: Ron and Honey contemplate laundering money through art at a Madison Avenue gallery opening in 1983.

Left: Ron Gonen and Mariel in the driveway of their Long Beach home, 1988. Gonen would routinely take Mariel on drug deals to deflect suspicion if he was stopped for traffic violations.

Right: Honey with newborn Mariel, Tel Aviv, 1985.

Below: Ron Gonen and Mariel in a Hershey, Pennsylvania motel room weeks before the family entered the Witness Protection Programme.

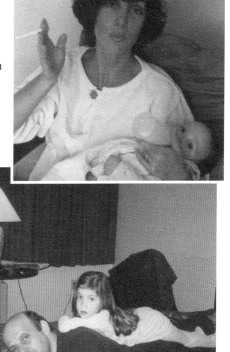

Left: Ron and Doris in Ron's Upper West Side apartment, September 1989 (shortly before his arrest).

Right:
Ran Ephraim, left, with Ron Gonen, right, Long Beach, 1989.

Above: Ron Gonen celebrates his sentencing with his wife, Honey Tesman, left, and his ex-wife, Doris Calle, right, 14 January 2000.

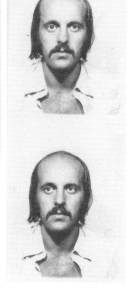

Above & Right:
Phoney passport photos used for
various heists.

Left: Honey's Honda
Prelude. The car was
blown up because of
Honey's connection
to the Lufthansa heist,
made famous in the
1991 movie *Goodfellas*.

Right: The Upper West
Side apartment Ron
Gonen rented through
most of the 1980s. He was
arrested in front of the
building on 27 September
1989.

Above: Surveillance photo of Ran Ephraim, January 1990.

Below: Surveillance photo of Ran Ephraim, January 1990.

Above: Surveillance photo of Ran Ephraim's wife, Judith, January 1990.

Below: Surveillance photo of Elia Ohana, January 1990.

Though it is impossible to know what happened during the twelve hours Soussan was kidnapped, the autopsy made it clear that he was tortured as Attias tried to get him to reveal where he was hiding the heroin. Soussan's body was found the next morning in the vicinity of Fountain Avenue, Seaview Avenue, and the Belt Parkway in Brooklyn. He had been shot once in the back of the head and once in the chest.

That afternoon, Attias took Ofra to the basement of their home and showed her a suitcase. In addition to Soussan's clothing—which Ofra recognised—the suitcase held women's clothing and other gifts. 'If you want something, take it,' Attias said. He had also taken a gold chain from Soussan's body, which he would later give to a girlfriend.

Ofra noted that the suitcase looked as if it belonged to Soussan, who she thought was her husband's friend.

'He will never celebrate Passover again,' Attias said.

The thought of her husband murdering Soussan bothered Ofra. By the time they went to bed that night, the discovery of his body had been reported on the news.

'Why kill him?' Ofra asked as they lay in their darkened bedroom. 'You could've broken his leg, you could've hurt him. But why kill him?'

'Because he turned out to be a fuck,' Attias said. 'He was an informant. He informed on me in Morocco.'

'If you wanted to do that, why did you take an audience with you?' Ofra said, referring to his three passengers. 'One day they might inform on you.'

'Don't worry,' Attias said. 'I let them do it ... they won't talk'.

The couple never talked about the murder again, but two days later while he was driving her from Queens to Brooklyn, Attias stopped the car in a deserted stretch of road. He got out for a moment and went into some bushes before returning to the car. It was too dark for Ofra to see what her husband had done, but the next day she overheard him telling Haya, Mizrachi, and Ran Ephraim that he had checked on something the previous night while driving with Ofra. They then joked about Soussan's murder.

Eitan Haya was developing a reputation as a cold-blooded killer. He had shot Soussan in an effort to gain favour with Attias, who recalled how Haya had seemed to enjoy torturing Soussan.

'You're bad,' Attias chuckled. 'How could you do it with such pleasure?'

Ran Ephraim relayed these stories to Gonen. He started dropping hints that Johnny Attias wanted Gonen to start dealing heroin in Manhattan so he could expand his power base. Gonen, hearing that Attias wanted him to join the so-called Israeli Mafia and hearing how much pleasure the core of the group took in killing others, felt sickened.

FOR THE MOST part, Gonen stayed in Manhattan and Long Beach, and Attias and his Israeli henchman stuck to running rackets in Queens and Brooklyn. Ephraim was the link between their two worlds. When they did see each other, Attias would hint that he wanted to know more about Gonen's steady cocaine business, and Gonen would try to distract him with talk about scores that didn't involve drugs.

Gonen suggested any crime that had a chance of distracting Johnny from his cocaine business, from robbing a Persian carpet dealer to simple burglaries. He knew how Attias worked—he'd demand a cut of whatever racket Gonen was running, and the cut would get bigger and bigger, forcing Gonen to take on riskier and riskier deals. His business was comfortable now. He dealt with people he knew and in quantities that would keep him on the shorter end of sentencing guidelines if he ever did get caught. If he started working with Attias, he knew it wouldn't be long before he'd also be dealing heroin by the kilo, something he wanted to stay away from.

'So I told him, "Fuck the drugs. Let's go for the stuff that's better than the drugs." And he liked the idea,' Gonen said. 'I knew he was the main animal, and I knew exactly how to talk to him, but I couldn't get him to go along with it .... The money with the heroin came every day, anytime you wanted it. The robberies involved planning.'

While Gonen pretended not to pick up on Attias' subtle hints, Ephraim showed that he was a full partner with Attias.

'You need to start brokering some bigger deals for me,' Ephraim finally told Gonen. 'I need to show these guys I can get and move cocaine *and* heroin.'

This is where it begins, Gonen thought. He was being sucked into Attias' world of contract killers and junkies. It was well known that Eitan Haya was already a heroin addict, and that the rest of Attias' crew—including Attias himself—were snorting the drugs they were importing from Amsterdam. The drug, however, hadn't mellowed his violent side. Once rumours about his double killing in Paris filtered through New York, Attias' ruthless reputation spread. But, for Attias, reputation wasn't enough to prove he would kill whoever crossed him.

When Attias heard about two low-level Italian gangsters dealing heroin in Queens, he felt as if his turf was being infringed. Attias arranged a meeting with the two dealers under the premise that he wanted to buy a couple of kilos. When the two men arrived, Attias was alone. They talked, made the deal, and then got comfortable, chatting and drinking in the empty Brooklyn warehouse. Then Attias shot them both before scooping up the heroin he had bought and the cash he had paid. He drove to Queens and knocked on the door of the Arab who had arranged the deal with the Italians. The man was startled by the night-time visit, but even more startled when he opened the door to find Attias pointing a gun in his face. Attias killed him. He retreated to an all-night diner where he flirted with a young waitress he would eventually date.

NOW JOHNNY ATTIAS had killed more than twice as many men in New York as he had in Paris. And here was Ephraim insisting that Attias had his and Gonen's best interests at heart.

'He's even set up bail guarantees,' Ephraim said. 'If anyone working with him gets busted, he pays their bail and then helps them flee back to Israel.'

Ephraim had always been a bit naïve, Gonen thought. To Gonen, it was obvious it would be much easier for Attias to kill someone who might potentially turn on him than go to the trouble of bailing him out and sending him back to Israel. At the same time, Gonen did not see how he could easily say no. Ephraim wanted Gonen to start putting together ten and 15-kilo cocaine deals. Profits from a cocaine trade would increase his value to the crew. 'If I don't start dealing cocaine for him, Johnny is just going to ask you directly,' Ephraim said.

The problem with the arrangement was that once Ephraim had purchased the kilos and shown them to Attias, Ephraim didn't have the connections to unload the blow. That left him turning to Gonen; in a sense, Ephraim was buying cocaine from Gonen and almost immediately selling some of it back to him at a $500 mark up. To Gonen, the mark up was insignificant— his brand of retail trade still meant he could buy a kilo for $25,000, cut it up and sell it for as much as $120,000.

Ephraim spent most days camped out in his room at the San Carlos Hotel, only occasionally leaving to meet Gonen at the apartment off of Columbus Avenue. Gonen called the apartment his 'secret place.' It was only really a secret from Honey Tesman, who had relapsed back into freebase cocaine addiction by the time Ephraim returned to New York in the summer of 1987. He never went out socially—if Gonen invited him out to dinner, Ephraim insisted on going someplace where they wouldn't have to spend more than $10 or $15 on a meal. More and more, he preferred hanging out with Attias. Attias' tastes were more in line with Ephraim's budget; Attias had adopted the Sea Dolphin, an inexpensive Kosher Italian restaurant on Coney Island Avenue in Brooklyn, as his crew's primary hangout.

EPHRAIM HAD LONG resisted Gonen's insistence that he wear suits or designer clothing when they went out in Manhattan, still preferring cargo pants, golf shirts, and combat boots. So on the day that Ephraim arrived at his secret place wearing one of the $500 warm-up suits that Johnny Attias preferred, Gonen knew that Ephraim now considered himself part of the crew.

'You look like an asshole,' Gonen told his friend.

'You're just a snob gangster,' Ephraim said. 'I'm comfortable.'

'Keep a suit in your car,' Gonen said. 'The next time you come into Manhattan to see me, you'll have something to change into.'

Gonen told him that the guys he was now dealing with were different than the crooks he had dealt with in the past. These were cold-blooded killers trying to take over Brooklyn and, eventually, all five boroughs. They were going to settle disputes with violence. Ephraim didn't want to hear it.

'At best, you end up running from a murder charge, and that never goes away,' Gonen said. 'At worst, you end up being the victim on the murder charge. And that definitely doesn't go away.'

'Johnny wouldn't do that to me,' Ephraim said. 'I make him too much money.'

They weren't going to agree, so Gonen told Ephraim he had to get ready to meet a friend at Elaine, an upscale Manhattan eatery. Ephraim asked if he could join them. 'Fine. But make sure you change your clothes,' Gonen said. He knew Ephraim would complain when the $500 lunch bill came, but he assured his friend he would like the restaurant and that it wouldn't be 'too expensive.' It wouldn't be too expensive by his standards, but would probably be more than Ephraim typically spent in a month of dining out.

A few hours later Gonen and his friend Avi were sitting in Elaine when Ephraim came in carrying a heavy briefcase. He strained to lug it to the table, and then set it on the floor with a thud. He sat down, never acknowledging the case or the sweat he had worked up walking from the cab to the table.

Ephraim wiped his brow with a napkin. Before they could ask him about the case, a waiter carrying a full tray of dishes tripped over it. The waiter fell and his tray of dishes crashed throughout the area surrounding their table. But the case had not moved. Ephraim started to apologise, thought better of it, and slid the case underneath their table.

'You have more than a couple of kilos in there,' Gonen said as he tapped the briefcase with his foot. 'What is it? A dead body?'

'Fuck you and mind your own business,' Ephraim said. 'I didn't have time to drop it off at my hotel.'

It was the start of a series of odd encounters that Gonen had with Ephraim. There had always been a competitive jealousy between them, but now Ephraim was becoming aloof. He dropped hints that Gonen could be making more money if he started working with Attias, but he didn't seem to rely on Gonen as he had once been. He spent most of his time in the hotel room, conducting quiet conversations on the black phone. And when he did go out, he headed to the Brooklyn dive bars Attias favoured.

Gonen decided his best option was to help Ephraim buy cocaine. It would buy him some time to get out of the drug business completely, and to figure out a more suitable solution before Attias could force him—at gunpoint—to join his crew. Attias would eventually figure out that it was Gonen, not Ephraim, who was moving all the cocaine, and he'd probably decide to cut Ephraim out as the middleman. He knew the arrangement wouldn't last long.

The more Gonen thought about his situation, the more helpless he felt. 'I'm going to need a miracle to get these guys off my back,' he complained to Honey Tesman.

That miracle never came. But Gonen did get something that bought him some more time with Attias and Ephraim: cancer.

8

COKE AND CANCER

SITTING IN THE kitchen of his Manhattan apartment one morning in the summer of 1988, Gonen noticed that one of his birthmarks had changed shape. Later that day he casually mentioned it to Avi.

Gonen had always referred to Avi as 'the doctor.' Avi himself wasn't a doctor, but he spent enough time with doctors to know that his friend should see one immediately. That afternoon, Gonen met with a doctor Avi had suggested. The next morning he had a biopsy. And by the following afternoon he had been diagnosed with malignant melanoma. Doctors scheduled outpatient surgery for the following week to remove the tumour.

If the diagnosis prompted Ran Ephraim to ease his pressure on Gonen to join the Attias crew, it did nothing to ease his reliance on Gonen to buy and sell cocaine. Just as Gonen was being diagnosed with cancer, Ephraim was increasing the size of his cocaine orders from the half- and one-kilo range to the five- and ten-kilo variety. On the day Gonen's tumour was being removed, Ephraim sat in the waiting room with five kilos of cocaine in a briefcase at his feet. His plan was to have Gonen take him to a buyer immediately following the procedure.

Gonen was exhausted but still went with Ephraim. He had no choice. Life was overwhelming at the moment, but the more he resisted Ephraim, the more Ephraim pressed. Saying yes to deliver five kilos now might mean he'd be able to say no to Ephraim when he asked him to deal heroin for Johnny Attias later. And when Ephraim wasn't riding him, Tesman was making him wonder if his cancer had been stress induced. She had used his diagnosis as an excuse to increase her cocaine consumption. When he did go home to the Long Beach house, he could not rest. If he went to his secret place on the Upper West Side or took a room at the Chelsea hotel, Ephraim would find him. He wanted nothing more than to have two or three days to sleep and mull over his grave diagnosis. But even in a city of 8 million people, there was no place to hide from Tesman or Ephraim.

And he still had to earn. Ephraim's sudden desire to buy more cocaine than he could sell meant Gonen was tapping out his usual suppliers. A fat restaurant owner named Eliot Danon ended up being the solution to both of Gonen's problems.

ELIESE ISRAEL DANON—known as Eliot in the United States—and Ron Gonen were introduced by a mutual friend early in 1988. They hit it off almost immediately. The two men shared the same birthday, 31 August, although Danon was nine years older than Gonen.

Both had operated in Germany for a while, and both had served time in German prisons: Gonen for fraud and burglary, Danon for highway robbery charges stemming from a hash deal gone bad. Danon knew Gonen's first wife, Doris Calle, and criminal mentor, Sammy Merckel.

Danon was not a picture of health. He was short—just 5 feet 4 inches tall—and bald, and counted eschemic heart disease, severe anginal syndrome, diabetes, and hyperlipidemia among his many ailments. He had horrible eyesight. He had spent most of his life working in the restaurant industry, and as a result, was prone to overeating. He smoked too much and, he told Gonen not long after they met, he liked to sample the cocaine that was running in and out of his restaurants. Most of Danon's friends and employees called him Poppa. When they met, Danon owned a small deli in Chelsea but was busy with plans to open a more upscale Italian restaurant.

Despite the long hours he put in at his restaurants, Danon was a good friend to Gonen. He gave him new cocaine customers and, eventually, a new cocaine connection that put Gonen one step away from a direct tie to a major cartel in Colombia. Perhaps most importantly, Danon gave Gonen free reign of the couch in his apartment at 17th Street and Fifth Avenue in Manhattan—a couch where Gonen could sleep and not worry about Tesman or Ephraim tracking him down.

They became each other's nursemaids. Gonen took care of Danon after he was discharged from St Vincent's Hospital following an angioplasty on 1 March 1988, and a follow-up on 3 May 1988. Danon let Gonen stay at his apartment following tumour operations in November and December of that same year.

Gonen was still buying most of his cocaine in a roundabout way from Ephraim. He knew it was a stupid setup that was costing him money, but it kept Ephraim happy. Gonen was finding more and more clients looking to do kilo-weight deals. Kilo deals involved less risk and less effort, but they also were marked by smaller margins. That extra $500 he was paying back to Ephraim could nearly erase his profit.

Alex Medlos, the Russian lounge singer, was buying as many as five kilos every month to smuggle to Berlin. Through a pot dealer named Reuben Perez—'Reuben the Cuban' in the underworld—Gonen met Michael Weatherby, a Connecticut carpenter who said he would buy fifteen kilos a month and pay $21,000 for each kilo he bought. Through Weatherby, Gonen met other kilo customers: a New Hampshire high school teacher who drove down to New York every few weeks to buy a couple of kilos, a Canadian serving time in an upstate New York prison who would drive into Manhattan while out for the day on work release. Hamilton Campos, a former Brazilian soccer star and kilo customer, introduced them to Billy Lutz. Lutz ended up buying a kilo from Gonen in Campos' New Jersey apartment every seven to ten days.

With Gonen conducting a good chunk of his business from a pay phone in Danon's restaurant, it wasn't long before Poppa made him an offer. Danon heard how much Gonen's Canadian and New Jersey clients were paying for each kilo and told Gonen he would beat whatever price Ephraim was charging him by $750.

'How?' Gonen said.

'Let's go talk to the Kid.'

'From that point on,' Gonen said later, 'I didn't need anybody else.'

Danon introduced Gonen to Jaime, a Colombian kid who did odd jobs for Danon. At the restaurant Jaime had several nicknames: Jimmy, the Kid, the Baby, the Boy, and the Soldier.

Jaime, Gonen would soon learn, had a friend named Rosita who had been sent to New York solely to distribute cocaine for the Medallion cocaine cartel. There were rumours about a warehouse in Queens where 250 kilos would arrive each month. It was a tempting target; Gonen briefly considered robbing the warehouse before learning the location changed every few weeks and was always patrolled by at least two heavily armed guards. Through Jaime, Danon agreed to broker kilo cocaine deals for Gonen, and would only take a $250 commission on each kilo for himself. That beat Ephraim's $500 commission and the base price was as much as $1,000 less than what Ephraim was paying.

Gonen needed the extra money. He didn't have health insurance, and he was raising a toddler, complete with frequent trips to the paediatrician. He was paying for Tesman's addictions and covering his own cancer treatments out of pocket. He would soon have massive holes in his budget. Even with his illness, he maintained expensive tastes—he often bragged to friends that he never returned home without having spent at least $500.

Beyond the low prices, Danon said, it was the highest quality cocaine running through New York. Indeed, Gonen knew almost immediately he had found a cocaine source worth holding onto. Colombians labelled their kilo bricks of cocaine, much like wine makers put labels on their bottles. They were postage stamp–sized stickers stuck to the plastic packaging wrapped around the brick. In those years Santana and Reina were two of the most sought after names in New York's cocaine economy. Rosita, Gonen quickly learned, was dealing exclusively in uncut Reina. Chances were if a person consumed Reina cocaine in the mid-1980s in New York City, Rosita had brokered the deal. Rosita, a classy woman in her mid forties, had a husband serving a life sentence in Florida and an 18-year-old son.

Through Jaime, Danon brokered the intricate arrangements of each exchange. Gonen bought himself and Rosita matching briefcases. He would fill his with cash and she would fill hers with cocaine. They would meet at a floral shop on the Upper East Side. Gonen was friends with the elderly owner and knew the man would have no idea a multi-kilo cocaine deal was being conducted as he carefully worked on a floral arrangement. He and Rosita would pretend they were strangers. She would ask him his opinion on a bouquet she was thinking of buying. For Gonen, it was a chance to practice his Spanish, which he hadn't used much since leaving Guatemala in late 1981. He would set his briefcase down next to hers, presumably to hold and examine the floral arrangement. They would talk casually, then each would leave with the other's briefcase.

By now, Ran Ephraim had grown suspicious that Gonen was cutting him out. Gonen stopped buying kilos back from him—for a while, Ephraim actually believed that Gonen's business was slowing down. After all, he had told Ephraim he had enrolled in night school in hopes of getting his realtor's license. Gonen dropped out of the 42-hour course after 39 hours when he learned that New York State only grants licenses to US citizens. But the 'business is slow' line only worked for so long, and in February 1988, Ephraim demanded a Friday afternoon meeting with Gonen in the bar of a midtown hotel.

Ephraim arrived with another heavy briefcase, the sixth or seventh Gonen had seen in the months leading up to the meeting. Gonen confessed. He told Ephraim about Danon, who Ephraim had met previously. He told him about the 24-year-old kid, Jaime, and his connection to Rosita. The quality of cocaine was better than what Israel Beck was shipping to Ephraim through Gonen, and Gonen now had his own list of kilo-weight customers.

Ephraim kept his anger in check but demanded that Gonen introduce him to Rosita. 'If she's that good, I want to deal with her, not Israel Beck,' Ephraim said. Gonen told Ephraim he would think about it. In a way, it was a relief to Gonen—he no longer had to hide the Reina cocaine from Ephraim and piece together enough connections to fill Ephraim's ever increasing cocaine orders. Still, he was wary of letting Ephraim into his private world.

'Have you thought anymore about dealing heroin for Johnny?' Ephraim said.

'No,' Gonen said. 'Because I'm not going to do it.'

Gonen made no secret that he considered heroin dealing a low-class line of work. He and Ephraim called cocaine 'uptown' and heroin 'downtown.' Attias, Eitan Haya, and Israel Alice had all come from the lower ranks of Israeli society and were used to dealing with deadbeats and junkies. Ephraim bragged, 'We have everyone—the niggers, the spics, and the Jews,' implying that Gonen would make more money if he expanded his customer base. Still he refused.

'You're too snobby for us?' Ephraim said. His faced flushed with anger. 'Why are you so picky?'

'Because you people always end up with dead bodies where you're walking,' Gonen said. 'You're talking about more than dealing heroin. You're talking about the electric chair.'

'There's going to come a point when you're not going to have a choice,' Ephraim said. 'Johnny won't take no for an answer forever.'

Ephraim stood to leave. He hoisted the briefcase and then drew close to Gonen. He looked him hard in the eye.

'If you had been a better friend,' Ephraim said, 'you would be a very rich man tomorrow morning.'

GONEN CHECKED INTO the Chelsea Hotel for the weekend. He needed someplace more comfortable and more fun than Danon's couch. He hadn't been staying at the Chelsea much recently, but he was still greeted warmly by the manager.

He stayed through Tuesday, 23 February. On that day he had breakfast in the lobby and read the newspaper. A small item on page 35 of that day's *New York Times* jumped out at him.

'Two Men Rob Jeweller of $4 Million in Gold,' the headline of the un-by lined article screamed. It was short—just three paragraphs—but gave details of the heist. A Diamond District jeweller, Raz Ben-Zvi, and his sister, Luiz, had been tied up by two masked men who forced their way into the Ben-Zvis' offices at 5.15pm the previous Friday—which, Gonen quickly noted, was around the same time Ephraim had arrived at the hotel bar with what would be the last of his heavy briefcases. The Ben-Zvis said the men had made off with $4 million in gold chains and jewellery and that they had been tied up until 9pm, when someone in a nearby office finally heard their cries for help.

'They suffered minor injuries as a result of being bound,' the article concluded.

Gonen knew how the scam had worked. Ephraim, after all, had staked his first trip to America with a similar—although far less lucrative—robbery at the Ben-Zvis' office. The briefcases had been full of gold bars that the Ben-Zvis had bought, claiming they would be melted down and cast into gold chains. But the bars were never shipped to their production facility. Instead they had been carted out by Ephraim in loads of 40 or 50 pounds every few days over a period of months. Ephraim had not been exaggerating when he told Gonen he had lost a chance to become a very rich man.

After the first sting, Ben-Zvi had used the insurance money to pay off the gold brokers who had sold him the gold on credit. But Johnny Attias had a different plan—he wanted to use the insurance cheques to turn a $4 million robbery into an $8 million heist. And Attias had no qualms about using force to carry out his plan.

The fact that he would be ripping off gold dealers with strong ties to the Italian Mafia did not deter him. For Attias, going head-to-head with the Italians was as good a way as any to prove the Israeli Mafia was real.

9

AFTERMATH

THEY WENT ON A spending spree.

Ran Ephraim fled to Brussels for a few months following the robbery, in part to sell the stolen gold he had not been able to move in the States. When he returned in the summer of 1988, he rented an apartment just two blocks away from Gonen's Long Beach home. Eitan Haya and Israel Alice bought expensive clothes and cars and began upping the amount of heroin they were buying—both to deal and to snort.

Johnny Attias, who had had little to do with the robbery, claimed the lion's share of the profits. He bought an expensive waterfront home in Oceanside and, to go along with his new property, a speedboat. The boat would become a source of constant frustration for Attias. After spending long afternoons during the summer of 1988 cruising and drinking in Long Island's Great South Bay, Attias would often fail to tie the boat off properly. The following morning's hangover would be interrupted by a shrill call from the Coast

Guard, reporting that they had found the boat drifting in the bay.

Gold is the ultimate black market commodity. It is nearly untraceable and holds its value. It can be melted down and made portable. Jewels, artwork, and antiques all lose value as soon as they are stolen. How many people want to pay a premium price for a stolen—and thus recognisable—painting? But when the *New York Times* reported that robbers had stolen $4 million in gold, the robbers did indeed make off with $4 million. The proceeds were split among Ephraim, Attias, and the Ben-Zvis, with merit cuts handed out to Haya and Israel Alice. But it wasn't enough for Attias. When Ephraim mentioned Raz Ben-Zvi had received the first of the insurance cheques in the fall of 1988, Attias saw the opportunity to double his wealth.

Attias knew that most of the people who had extended credit to Ben-Zvi were small mom-and-pop gold brokers. Because Ben-Zvi had spread his business through several different gold brokers, each broker would only be out a few hundred thousand dollars— hardly an amount of money worth pursuing in court or through collection agencies, if it meant losing your life.

At first, the plan worked flawlessly. Ben-Zvi would place a panic-stricken call to Ephraim whenever some of his associates grew impatient with his failure to repay. News that Ben-Zvi had received his insurance cheques spread quickly through the Diamond District, and the calls came in rapid succession.

'I can't just not pay them,' Ben Zvi pleaded.

'I'll take care of it,' Ephraim said.

Ephraim called Attias, who sent Eitan Haya, Israel Alice, or another pair of toughs to visit the jeweller demanding payment. The message was violently clear: If they so much as thought of pursuing Ben-Zvi in court or placing another call to Ben-Zvi's Josi Jewellery offices, they would be killed. Painfully. The tactic was sure to ruin Ben-Zvi's business—the jewellery industry is small and tightly knit, and no one in their right mind would ever do business with him again—but Ephraim and Attias assured him with his cut of the extra $4 million in insurance money, he wouldn't need to work.

'I'm going to jail,' Ben-Zvi groaned.

'No one is going to jail,' Ephraim said. 'If it gets to that point—and it won't—Johnny will bail you out and sneak you back to Israel.'

The law enforcement pressure would come later. Soon it became clear there was a miscalculation in the Attias plan with more immediate consequences. Attias hadn't taken into account that just as Ben-Zvi had ties to the Israeli Mafia, many of the brokers they were robbing had close bonds to the Italian Mafia.

In 1988, the five crime families that made up New York's Italian Mafia were on the verge of an internal gang war. But there was certainly time to deal with a handful of Israelis who were getting too big for their own good. Hours after Israel Alice and Eitan Haya had visited a jeweller with ties to the Colombo crime family, threats started flying across Brooklyn. A group of Italians showed up at one of Attias' offices, beating up the employees and overturning desks and filing cabinets. Ephraim fretted to Gonen that Attias was psychotic enough to take on the Italians. He was visibly relieved when he told Gonen that Attias had agreed to a sit down with Frankie 'The Bug' Sciortino, a high-ranking capo in the Colombo family.

FOR HIS PART, Ephraim was eager to spend some of the money he had earned with the first round of profits from the Ben-Zvi bust. When he returned to the United States, he told Gonen he wanted to start brokering large-scale cocaine deals through Rosita. Gonen agreed to introduce Ephraim first to Danon and Jaime—then, if they were comfortable with him, Rosita.

Ephraim immediately despised Danon. He was sickly and out of shape—'weak' was how Ephraim would describe him to Gonen after the meeting. Ephraim reluctantly offered to pay Danon a $250 commission on each kilo he purchased through Rosita. Danon saw the low figure as an insult.

'He just wants to get comfortable,' Gonen said. 'I'm sure he'll raise it once things get going. Besides, he said he's going to be buying a lot of product, so that $250 can add up quickly.' Gonen never mentioned that his own commission from Ephraim—simply for introducing him to Danon and riding shotgun on the exchanges—was $500 per kilo. In 1988 and 1989, Danon brokered deals for a total of 79 kilos with both Gonen and Ephraim, collecting more than $19,000 on the transactions.

Ephraim started relatively small, buying a total of four kilos from Rosita in two separate deals. Convinced the quality of the product was good and the price was fair, Ephraim went ahead and placed an order for fifteen kilos through Danon. He said he had a buyer named Pistoleiro who was looking to move large quantities of cocaine.

Gonen was constantly nervous being the middleman between Ephraim and Rosita. Rosita had been his perfect connection: low prices, easy transactions, and a seemingly uninterrupted supply. He worried—and for good reason, as it turned out—that Ephraim would do something to ruin his connection.

The transactions were conducted in a cloak-and-dagger fashion in the streets around Rosita's apartment. She would take the elevator in her building to the street while carrying the cocaine in a briefcase. Once they made eye contact, Gonen would get out of Ephraim's car and walk a briefcase full of cash to a waiting car. That car sped off and a few moments later—presumably after the money had been counted and a signal had been sent to Rosita—she would emerge from the lobby of the building and drop the briefcase full of cocaine into Ephraim's car. Gonen was so paranoid that Ephraim would betray Rosita that he tried to secretly count the money before each deal.

Despite his worries, the deals were a good move for Gonen. It was easy work. In some of Ephraim's heavier weeks, Gonen could make $20,000 just for counting a briefcase full of money and walking it to a car where Jaime was waiting.

Naturally, it wouldn't last. The uneasy truce between Danon and Ephraim started to unravel in November. Surprisingly, it was the meek Danon who fired the first salvo.

'This is bullshit,' Danon told Ephraim and Gonen one afternoon in Danon's apartment. 'You need to up my commission.'

Ephraim was stunned that Danon would speak to him so forcefully. Gonen put his head in his hands. Ephraim had spent enough time with Attias that year that Gonen was unsure if Ephraim would remain rational.

'You're lucky you're getting anything, you stupid motherfucker,' Ephraim said. 'You don't do shit. I could kill you. Instead I give you $250 a key just for being fat.'

The tension held but the immediate rage of the moment passed. When they left, Ephraim told Gonen he needed to work out a deal with Rosita and Jaime to cut Danon out.

'Jaime won't go for that,' Gonen said. 'He and Eliot are tight. Tighter than you and me.'

'What does that mean?'

'You would cut me out of a deal if Jaime came and asked you to do it,' Gonen said. 'But Jaime won't cut Eliot out. He's like a father to him.'

'Well, cut them both out,' Ephraim said. 'Talk to Rosita. I'll give you their cut.'

'Rosita isn't going to cut Jaime out,' Gonen said. 'You're already getting a good deal. I don't see why you want to fuck it all up.'

'Because I don't like Eliot,' Ephraim said.

It was more than Gonen wanted to deal with. He was scheduled for a second tumour operation the following week and had spent most of the year convinced he was dying of cancer. After the operation, he was scheduled to take a vacation with Tesman, Mariel, and Tesman's daughter to Atlantic City to recuperate. Recuperation—in a hotel room with Tesman and her freebase pipe—would be impossible. To further complicate the vacation, Ephraim was planning to run an eight-kilo deal with Rosita during that week when both Gonen and Danon were out of town. It would be up to Gonen to collect both of their commissions, which would be hard enough if he were along for the deal.

As Gonen suspected, Ephraim screwed Danon on the deal. What he hadn't suspected is that Ephraim would screw him as well.

They were halfway through their Atlantic City vacation when Ephraim called to say the deal had gone off without any problem. He said he had left an envelope with the owner of the deli across the street from Gonen's apartment in Manhattan.

'There's $5,000 in it,' Ephraim said.

'So you're going to pay Eliot when he gets back from Israel?' Gonen said. 'Right?'

The math wasn't lost on Gonen: with his $4,000 commission and Danon's $2,000 commission, the envelope was $1,000 short.

'It's up to you on whether or not you want to pay Eliot,' Ephraim said. 'You can pay him out of that if you think he deserves it.'

Gonen was silent.

'Oh, and you'll need to give Rosita $3,000 of that $5,000,' Ephraim said.

'What the fuck?'

'The briefcase was $3,000 short—in case the product wasn't good,' Ephraim said.

'So if I screw Eliot, I get a $250 commission?' Gonen said.

'You didn't do anything. Eliot didn't do anything,' Ephraim said. 'You weren't even here. I didn't think I needed to give you anything. So Happy Hanukkah.'

FOR RON GONEN, 1989 started as badly as it would end.

In January, not too long after the family returned from Atlantic City, Honey Tesman had a nervous breakdown. With the help of her sisters, Gonen was able to get her admitted into a drug rehabilitation programme. Now caring for his three-and-a-half-year-old daughter, the last person Gonen needed to hear from was Ephraim—especially after Ephraim had stiffed him and Danon out of their full commissions on the eight-kilo deal.

Danon was still in Israel, and Ephraim needed to make another eight-kilo cocaine deal. But he couldn't get in touch with Jaime. Gonen called Rosita, who was evasive.

'Something happened, but you don't need to know about it,' Rosita said. 'Let's just say Jaime is in a lot of trouble.'

The mystery was solved two nights later when Jaime appeared at Gonen's apartment. He was badly beaten and had clearly been awake for several days.

Jaime told Gonen that he had been accused of stealing 20 kilos and $100,000 in jewels from Rosita. He had been taken to a warehouse in Queens and beaten. The Colombians holding him said that he would be beaten until he told them where he had hidden the jewels and what he had done with the cocaine. The problem, Jaime said, was that he hadn't stolen the cocaine or the jewels and had no idea what had happened to them. He finally managed to escape and, not knowing where else to go, he had gone to Gonen's apartment.

'I need a gun,' Jaime said.

Gonen cringed and felt stress knot his stomach. On one side he had Johnny Attias playing a game of chicken with the Colombo crime family and sending increasingly less gentle hints that he needed to start dealing heroin. Now the Colombians—his prized cocaine source and the maker of profits that had allowed him to stave off Attias' demands—were unravelling in some sort of bizarre civil war. And Eliot Danon, the one person who could talk to both Rosita and Jaime, was still in Israel.

'I need a gun,' Jaime repeated.

'I'm not giving you a gun,' Gonen said. 'You can stay here until Eliot gets back, until things calm down a bit.'

And then Gonen did the only thing he could think to do: He left. He drove straight to the empty Long Beach house. If the Colombians were able to track down Jaime at Gonen's apartment, Gonen did not want to be there when they found him.

When Tesman was released from the rehab, Gonen didn't give her much time away from drugs. He had no choice—he needed to make money quickly, and the

quickest way he could think of making money was to
have her start carting kilos to Europe.

10

HIGH STAKES POKER

LUCK CHANGES FAST in the underworld.

For Michael Markowitz, a thick-jowled Russian gangster who liked to be called the 'Jewish Scarface,' the night had started with promise. He was winning a poker game hosted by his business partner and long time friend Yosef 'Joe' Reich. Markowitz kept pulling aces and greedily dragging chips toward himself. When he leaned forward, the gold chains dangling from his thick neck made him look more like a white Mr T than the Hollywood Cuban cocaine cowboy he admired. Markowitz loved being a self-declared wiseguy.

Johnny Attias and Israel Mizrachi played cards with Markowitz that night but soon decided they'd had enough of watching him take their chips. They got up to leave at midnight. Markowitz played for another 30 minutes before he cashed out and collected $1,000 in winnings. Not bad for a friendly weeknight game. He stuffed the bills into the breast pocket of his tailored sharkskin suit, stepped outside of Reich's

Mill Basin home, and headed to his silver-and-maroon Rolls Royce.

If Markowitz was bothered by the events of recent months—the murder of an associate, the word 'Rat' being spray painted in thick black letters on some of the more than two hundred gas stations he owned, or the constant pleas of the FBI agents handling his case to enter the Witness Protection Programme—he did not show it as he lumbered down Reich's walkway. Luck had always been on his side. A decade earlier he had arrived from Romania with nothing. He had scraped together enough money to buy his first gas station and rigged the pumps to charge a few extra pennies for every gallon he sold. He'd become rich through a 'daisy chain' gasoline scam that allowed him to skim millions of dollars in state taxes from the service stations he owned in Brooklyn and Queens. He started most mornings by going to his office and counting stacks of bills—many of them still smelling of gasoline—in a conference room. In an average month, he pocketed $1.5 million, tax-free. Several years earlier he had partnered with La Cosa Nostra in the scam. It was a relationship that had only recently turned rocky when Michael Luchese, his Colombo family contact, was arrested and agreed to testify against his former associates. Still, Markowitz was tied to the Italians. He had nothing to fear.

What he didn't know was that those same Italians he counted on for protection had tried to kill him on his last visit to the neighbourhood, when he had stopped for breakfast at a favourite Brooklyn bagel shop. The only thing that had saved him was that both the driver and gunman hired by Colombo family capo Frankie 'The Bug' Sciortino had fallen asleep in the car while waiting for Markowitz.

But Markowitz didn't know this. He was feeling lucky from a good night of poker as he started his car and turned onto East 66th Street. He hadn't even travelled a third of a mile when he saw a pair of brake lights blocking his way. Two men stepped out of a black BMW, and, for a moment, Markowitz panicked. But when he saw what they were wearing—warm-up suits—Markowitz recognised the men and relaxed. One man headed to the driver's side, and Markowitz rolled down the window. The other man remained standing next to the passenger side of the BMW.

Markowitz started to speak but then noticed the .38 calibre revolver in his friend's hand. 'Fuck!' he said in Russian.

The man fired twice and two bullets lodged in Markowitz's chest. His car lurched forward and smashed into a Buick parked near the curb. Markowitz swung the door open and staggered out of the car. He spun on one foot, as if looking for assistance from the other man, who was still standing by the passenger's door of the BMW and calmly smoking a cigarette. The gunman fired again, this time hitting Markowitz under his right shoulder blade.

'Let's go!' the smoker hissed in Hebrew.

The shooter slid the gun into the pocket of his warm-up suit and ran back to the car. The BMW sped off with a squeal of the tires, heading for Queens. Markowitz was still alive. He wailed as he crawled to one of the stoops lining the normally quiet, residential street.

Neighbours initially thought Markowitz was drunk. It was only when a neighbourhood security guard happened by did they begin to realise the problem was much more serious. They knew who Markowitz was. Up until a few months ago, he had lived in this neighbourhood, and his parents still lived nearby in a $400,000 house he had bought for them.

Markowitz was able to name his killers, but the panic mixed with his thick Russian accent made the words unintelligible. 'Kind of foreign sounding,' was the best one witness could recall later on. Then Markowitz offered a reward to anyone in the gathering crowd who killed the shooters.

'I'll pay you whatever you want,' he said as he was lifted into an ambulance.

They would be his last words; Markowitz died on his way to Kings County Hospital.

'Just like Markowitz,' said one Brooklyn lawyer. 'He thought he could buy and sell anybody, right up to the end.'

Even if Markowitz had lived to make good on his offer, the line-up of potential killers was both long and intimidating. Sciortino still wanted Markowitz dead, but it seemed unlikely that the Colombos would have been able to find Markowitz in this neighbourhood. And even if they had, they would never send someone here to kill him. There were also long-standing rumours that Markowitz had stolen $9 million from Reich. But Reich wasn't stupid enough to ambush Markowitz so close to his own home, especially on a night the two men had played cards together. Even John Gotti, the gossips said, had marvelled at Markowitz's gas scam. He had marvelled at it so much that he had reportedly considered eliminating Markowitz as a competitor.

'It could've been anybody who ever met him,' one former associate said. 'He went just a little too far with the free enterprise system.'

Indeed, it could have been anyone. But what no one suspected was why Markowitz knew his killers and why he was able to offer up their names so readily. Markowitz knew his killers' names because he had played poker with them that very night.

2 MAY STARTED like most other mornings for Ron Gonen. His wife was still a mess, a junkie in the throes of a lifelong drug addiction. That spring he had been spending even more time than usual in his Manhattan apartment. It was a well-appointed, fourth-storey walk-up, and it was quiet here. Gonen had all but conceded their Long Beach home to Honey Tesman, only visiting to spend time with Mariel or to arrange Tesman's next trip overseas to deliver coke to Berlin.

By now, Tesman was more of a mule than a wife. About once a month, Gonen would send her to Germany with a kilo or two of high-quality cocaine he had purchased for $16,000 or less. In Berlin, Tesman would drop off the drugs with one of his contacts and take a return flight to New York—hopefully with most of the $60,000 in profits intact. The money went to his ongoing cancer treatments and, hopefully, to get Gonen out of dealing cocaine. He also hid enough of it away so that if he did indeed die, either by cancer or by Johnny Attias, Tesman would have some money to raise Mariel.

Tesman liked to pose as a pregnant woman on the trips. The kilos could be tucked into the fake belly she was wearing, and her condition meant extra attention from the flight attendants. Tesman loved attention. And no one ever questioned a pregnant woman's frequent visits to the small airplane lavatory. No one ever suspected that each of those trips was a chance to stick a silver straw into the pile of loose cocaine she kept in her purse.

It wasn't the best arrangement. She had nearly been caught once, only getting out of the jam when she flirted with the German customs official who had spotted the cocaine in her purse. And the kilos were never full kilos by the time they got to Frantz, Gonen's connection in Europe. But it was the only arrangement that Gonen had, and with the New York drug market being as tight as it was, the risk was worth the potential payoff.

On 2 May, Gonen returned to the apartment from the 10th Street Baths around noon. The pagers he used for his coke dealing would not begin chirping until later that afternoon. He had three, maybe four hours of kill time that he planned to use by calling his connections to see if there were any leads on product. Following a one-ton bust earlier that year in Queens, demand had far outstripped supply, and Gonen was having trouble meeting the needs of the Canadians, Germans, and coke-crazy New Yorkers in his social circle.

Drug dealing has a language unto itself. If Gonen's contact said, 'The girls are in New York,' it would be good news, as each 'girl' was a kilo of Colombian cocaine ready for pickup somewhere in the area. But if the girls were '16-and-a-half-years-old,' it meant they were pricey—$16,500—as well. 'They're too old,' he would tell whatever connection he was dealing with on that particular day.

But even 16-and-a-half-year-old girls were starting to seem reasonable. Girls were scarce as the drought dragged on. Even the Colombians were dry. Gonen was frantic in his efforts to piece together quality product. Johnny Attias and Ran Ephraim, who dealt mostly with freebasers and crack addicts, didn't care about quality when it came to cocaine. It didn't matter if it reeked of kerosene or had that ugly, yellow tinge of old product cut several times—they would buy it and sell it anyway.

But for Gonen, quality was everything. His retail trade was still primarily made up of musicians, night clubbers, and models, the uptown clientele who liked to spend a lot of money on their drugs, the people who liked to snort it and the people who did not expect an aftertaste or worse with each line they ingested. And the men buying cocaine by the kilo from him wanted nothing but pure, high-quality cocaine.

Ephraim and Attias didn't care about the quality of their 'uptown' product because, more and more, they had been dealing in 'downtown' heroin, which was on the verge of making a resurgence in New York City drug culture. Attias was still determined to be at the forefront of the fad. He bought kilos of heroin from an

Amsterdam dealer he called The Turk. For $30,000 and a willingness to accept the risk of smuggling the drug back to New York, Ephraim, Attias, and their crew would have a kilo that could be broken up and sold for $300,000 in Brooklyn. And if heroin could fetch $300,000 per kilo on the streets of Brooklyn, they reasoned that if they could turn Gonen's upscale Manhattan coke users onto the drug, their earning potential would be limitless.

The problem was, Gonen still didn't want anything to do with it.

GONEN HEARD THE pounding of footsteps in the stairwell outside the door of his apartment. Only one person took steps two at a time when he came to visit him here, and that person was now sprinting up the stairs to his apartment.

Ephraim.

Gonen cracked the door, expecting another round of pressure in Ephraim's persistent effort to bring him into the fold. His buddy Ran, who would make fun of him, call him a snob gangster and remind him how he had missed his chance earlier that year to be in on the $8 million gold robbery. Ephraim, who was drifting further and further away as a friend and closer and closer to Attias.

'That motherfucker!' Ephraim screamed in Hebrew as he burst through the half-opened door and into Gonen's apartment. 'He borrowed my car and he killed a guy!'

Panic spilled into the room with Ephraim. He was normally tanned, and, after running up four flights of stairs, usually ruddy. But not today. Today, Gonen immediately noticed, he was ashen white.

'He killed Markowitz! He used my car!' Ephraim stammered. Gonen knew immediately that 'he' was Johnny Attias.

Through a series of nervous starts, stops, and rage-filled tangents, Ephraim was able to tell the story. The previous night, Attias had borrowed the black BMW that Gonen had helped Ephraim buy just a few months earlier. He told Ephraim he was going to play poker in Mill Basin. But what he hadn't told him until that morning was that he was using the car to carry out a hit commissioned by the Colombo crime family. Attias assured him that following the ambush they had sped away before anyone could get a description of the automobile, but Ephraim wasn't so sure.

Gonen knew that a few weeks earlier Ephraim, Johnny Attias, and Israel Alice had had a sit-down with a high-ranking capo in the Colombo family. It had taken place at the Queens Boulevard Diner, which would become popular a couple of years later as a set in the movie *Goodfellas*. There had been a series of fights and skirmishes between Italians and Israelis in the New York jewellery business in the aftermath of the Ben-Zvi robbery. The fights, Gonen had been told, stemmed from the distribution of the insurance money between Diamond District jewellers.

In the weeks that followed, Ephraim had been letting details of the meeting slip into their frequent talks. It had been big for the Israelis, he assured Gonen, a coming of age for a gang that hadn't even existed just four years earlier. Gonen was able to surmise that the failure of Israeli jewellers to give insurance money to the Italians had been forgiven at the sit-down. Ephraim bragged that during the meeting Attias had convinced the Italians to rent him a warehouse near JFK Airport, a massive mark of acceptance in the underworld. But another part of the conversation had gone unmentioned by Ephraim until this moment: The Colombos had asked Johnny and Mizrachi to kill Markowitz. In return, the two men would receive $25,000.

The Colombos, Ephraim now explained, were worried that with Luchese in custody, other players in the Daisy Chain scam would be arrested. Markowitz, who bragged about his frequent meetings with FBI agents and claimed he fed them false information, was seen as the most likely to talk. He was a Russian, exempt from the rules of *Omerta* and a big liability. Having failed to track him down in Mill Basin, the Colombos hired Attias, who knew the neighbourhood well and was close with Markowitz's underworld associates.

Gonen's face flushed as the implications dawned on him. The fresh murder was coming shortly after Attias had killed two Italians and their Arab drug supplier in cold blood. It was coming after a pattern of increasingly erratic and brazen behaviour. Gonen felt like he was the only one who could see that they would all end up in jail or dead.

The story ended with Attias and Israel Alice speeding away in Ephraim's BMW. 'You should get a good lawyer,' Gonen told Ephraim. 'You're dealing with a mad dog. What are you going to do?'

Ephraim, who had initially come to Gonen looking for advice, became defensive. He pointed out that Johnny Attias was now firmly aligned with the Italians—they had asked him to do something, and he had done it perfectly.

'Nothing will happen to us,' Ephraim said. 'Now we have increased our own value.'

Gonen had a sudden moment of clarity. Ephraim was insinuating that Johnny Attias was now unstoppable, and Gonen's efforts to resist dealing heroin needed to end. Though he never mentioned it directly, Ephraim was no doubt counting on the fact that the fresh murder would show Gonen that Attias didn't care who he murdered if it bolstered his bottom line.

'I'm screaming to myself 'It's murder!' He's basically trying to tell himself that he's doing right,' Gonen would later recall. 'And I'm thinking I need to get out.'

The risk Ephraim was taking didn't make sense to Gonen. He knew that at any given time Ephraim had between $800,000 and $1 million in cash in a Manhattan safe deposit box. He knew a large hunk of the $8 million from the gold robbery had gone to Ephraim. His best estimate at that time was that Ephraim's liquid value was somewhere between $4 million and $5 million.

'Why are you doing this?' Gonen said. 'Is it about the money or the power?'

'It's not about the money,' Ephraim said. 'It's about the power. It's to belong.'

The blood rushed back to Ephraim's face as he stood and glared at Gonen.

'You need to choose what type of gangster you want to be,' Ephraim said.

'I want to be anything but what you and Johnny have become,' Gonen said. 'I don't need to walk into a restaurant and have the first five drinks for free because my name is my name and I did it with muscle.'

Ephraim turned to leave. Get out, Gonen said to himself as the apartment door closed behind Ephraim. Get out of this business, get out of this city and get away from these people, he told himself.

But getting out would take money. He would need to step up the number of trips Tesman was making to Europe. He also knew that he could stave off Ephraim for just a little bit longer; if he could show him there was still plenty of money to be made in cocaine. But both tracks required large quantities of quality product, something Gonen hadn't had access to for months.

If it seemed too good to be true when Hamilton Campos called and said he had a line on 200 14-year-old girls from Brazil, it probably was.

11

DIVISIVE ACTIONS

ON THE SURFACE, it looked like what Johnny Attias had said it was: a hit commissioned by the Italian Mafia.

Attias even had $25,000 from the Italians, which he handed out to people who had helped him on the hit: Israel Alice, who had driven the car and fired the shots, and Ran Ephraim, who had provided the black BMW. Attias even bought the car from Ephraim and registered it in his own name in an effort to allay Ephraim's fears.

But Ofra Attias knew otherwise, and in the weeks that followed the murder, it became clear to almost everyone involved that Johnny Attias had no interest in building ties with the Italians. Before the murder, Attias told Ofra he was working on some arrangements for Yosef 'Joe' Reich's brother-in-law, Steve Steigel-fest. He told her he was going to get the Italian 'Mafia out of the gasoline business.' Indeed, in the weeks following the murder, Reich—who had been Markowitz's partner—started paying Attias $1,500 a week. The amount later increased to $5,000 a week.

Within an hour after Mizrachi shot Markwoitz, Attias called Ofra and told her that Ran Ephraim would be stopping by to take some items from their home. Ephraim arrived at 3am and carted out Ofra's handbag, Attias' guns, a pound of marijuana, and scales used for weighing drugs. Ephraim didn't say much to Ofra, but she could tell that something had gone wrong. At the same time Ephraim was at Attias' house, Attias and Mizrachi were at Ephraim's house changing their blood-spattered clothes.

When Johnny had still not returned home by 5am, Ofra began making a series of frantic phone calls. Steigelfest told her he had not seen her husband all night. Ran Ephraim—who was presumably still hiding the items he had removed from her home—did not answer. Ofra knew Attias had a girlfriend, a woman named Semadar who she called 'the Worm.' Ofra grew angry as she thought of her husband spending the night with Semader.

Attias finally came home to his wife at 6am, looking exhausted. Ofra was furious when she saw he was driving a white car—just like the Worm's car—but on closer inspection she saw it was Joe Reich's white Mercedes. It was typical for Attias to return home with money each evening, and Ofra would count it and hide it for her husband. On this night, the amount was extraordinary: Ofra spent nearly an hour counting some $80,000. Attias would later tell her it was the $25,000 the Italians had paid to eliminate Markowitz, as well as the money Reich had kicked in for the hit.

Later that morning a string of visitors arrived at the house. Israel Mizrachi showed up, as did Elio

Hana and Ran Ephraim. Ephraim would eventually explain to Ofra that Markowitz had been killed with the blessing of the Italians who, like Joe Reich, feared that Markowitz was talking with federal prosecutors. Beyond that, Reich was sleeping with Markowitz's wife, Lea. The affair became more open after her husband's murder.

It was a coming of age for the Israeli Mafia, but it wasn't a celebratory moment. Ephraim, as he later told Gonen, was mad that they had used his car, but he wasn't the only one who was upset. While Reich had concocted the idea to ambush Markowitz after a poker game at his home, he was now concerned over how close the spot Attias selected was to his driveway. Israel Alice would later complain to Ofra, 'Your husband went in as partner in the gas and what did I get out of this? I got peanuts.'

The men continued to discuss the murder throughout the morning. They talked about how Markowitz had begged for his life and crashed his car. They were jittery and nervous, and tempers flared. Mizrachi got angry and accused Attias of calling him by name at the murder scene. To calm him down, Attias handed him a small stack of $100 bills.

At the same time, Attias belittled Mizrachi. He berated him for bringing just three bullets to the hit. Mizrachi sheepishly explained he had used the rest of the bullets in the gun shooting another man at the Mirpeset nightclub a few days earlier.

Noticeably absent during all of the commotion at the Attias house in the days following the Markowitz hit was Eitan Haya. But that didn't mean he wasn't angry.

EITAN HAYA WAS always a bit of an outsider in the Israeli Mafia. When Ran Ephraim and Israel Mizrachi were operating in Paris and the Middle East, waiting for Johnny Attias to be released from prison, Haya had already moved to Queens. He moved there after serving ten years of a life sentence for murder in Israel. Even sketchier than the details of the murder are the details of his release: Court papers and Interpol rap sheets only offer that he was released by 'presidential order' in 1981 or 1982.

Haya did not share Attias' rugged good looks. He was 5 feet 2 inches tall and wore boots to give him some lift. But he had managed to marry an incredibly attractive woman; she was so beautiful that it wasn't long before rumours circulated through the group that Attias was sleeping with Haya's wife. The couple had a son, Aaron, who was born in 1983, not long after Haya was released from prison and just before he moved his family to New York.

Attias and Haya had initially hit it off. Attias viewed Israel Mizrachi as a loyal henchman but too stupid to be trusted with complex tasks and decisions. And while Attias frequently went to Ephraim for counsel, Ephraim wasn't a hardened killer like Attias or Haya. He hadn't proven himself or shown a capacity for doing the gang's dirtier work. Besides, Ephraim was a gossip; while Attias coveted Ron Gonen's abilities to sell drugs and move product, Attias worried that Ephraim told Gonen too much about their other activities.

At first they were natural counterparts. Haya helped Attias track down Albert 'Beber' Soussan and even went along for the all-night torture spree in April 1988, which ended with Haya shooting Soussan and dumping his body on a deserted Brooklyn street. Around the same time, Haya helped Attias put together the multimillion-dollar hashish deal which gave them seed money for a string of criminal activities that established the Israeli Mafia in New York City.

But if they were natural counterparts, they were also natural opposites. Haya didn't like the idea of pushing into the Italian Mafia's turf, but he also didn't like the idea of being kept out of the loop—particularly when money was involved. Court documents describe him as being visibly upset when he heard about the payoff for the Markowitz murder because he had not been included. Later that summer, Haya and Attias began bickering over their loan sharking business, with Attias accusing Haya of trying to push him out of the racket by stealing his clients. By September, Haya had told other members of the Israeli Mafia he feared that Attias was going to kill him.

Attias tried to assure Haya that they were still friends and that no one would kill anyone. And then he immediately went out and deliberately made sure Haya was cut out of one of the gang's biggest drug scores to date: a four kilo heroin deal that, when it had all been sold off, was worth $1.2 million.

In the summer of 1989, Attias, Ephraim, Mizrachi, and three other men began concocting a plan to smuggle four kilograms of heroin from Holland to the United States. They recruited a seventh, Elio Hana, as their courier. Hana had been a policeman in Israel and portrayed himself as Johnny Attias' bodyguard. He was 41 and was selected to make the trip because he was the only member of the group who had a US passport.

He was also crazy, but that helped when doing something as nerve-racking as flying more than a million dollars worth of heroin into the United States in a carry-on bag.

Attias knew he could purchase kilos in Amsterdam and from Southeast Asia, bring them to New York, cut them up, and move them on the streets for ten times what he had paid for them. But there were no established supply routes: Up until now, he had been moving drugs from Amsterdam much the same way Ron Gonen had moved them to Israel a few years earlier—no more than a half kilo a time. Attias wanted to flood the New York market with cheap heroin, and he knew the only way to do that was to take a chance— or, more accurately, have Hana take a chance.

Attias, Ephraim, and Mizrachi, who had invested the lion's share of money to purchase the drug, talked about Hana's trip as being an act of 'suicide.' But the plan was simple—and stupid—enough that it might actually work.

More than a year after the deal, Ofra would remember the weeks leading up to the deal as being tense. She recalled her husband arguing over the telephone with Ran Ephraim, who was in Holland brokering the deal. While the package Hana would deliver would weigh less than two pounds, it was an astronomically large amount of heroin—particularly in

1989, a few years before heroin replaced cocaine as the hard drug of choice on the global market. Beyond that, Attias was insisting that the drug not be cut; he wanted to do that himself, once it was safely back in the study of his Long Island home. During that period, Israel Alice was a constant fixture at the Attias household, sometimes stopping by two, three, or even four times a day to inquire about the status of the deal. With the passage of time since the Markowitz hit, Israel Alice realised he was not going to get caught, and he eased back into his comfortable friendship with Attias.

Ephraim arrived at Attias' house with his wife Judith early on the day Hana was due to return from Holland. The men—who would eventually be joined by Israel Alice and the other three partners on the deal—were keyed up and jumpy. Everyone was outright relieved, and then overwhelmingly happy, when Hana walked into Attias' living room at the appointed time, carrying a dark-coloured handbag made of soft material. Ofra took the bag and moved it into Attias' study while the men talked about Hana's trip. Later all six men retreated to the study to begin the process of cutting and dividing the heroin among themselves. Judith and Ofra stayed in the living room. Occasionally someone would leave the study and go to the kitchen to retrieve a bowl, plastic bags, or an extra scale.

After everyone had left, Attias told Ofra to clean all of the bowls and get rid of any heroin residue. He and Ephraim spent the next several hours burying their share of the heroin in Attias' garden. They had broken the heroin into several smaller bags and Attias assumed it would be safer to store the drugs outside of the house until it could all be sold off. He was starting to come under suspicion for a variety of crimes, in New York and was constantly paranoid that any day a law clerk would type up a search warrant for his home.

It is not clear how much Hana was paid to act as the courier, but his actions after he returned suggest he felt that he should have been paid more—and his next move proved that he was indeed crazy. What he did next was decide to rip off Johnny Attias. Hana also complained to Eitan Haya—who, by now, was furious that he had not been included in the deal—that he felt like Attias had demoted him to a common courier. It was a huge step down for a man who used to take pride in accompanying Attias on murders and helping him plan major scores; Hana felt he had been replaced in those two capacities by Israel Alice and Ephraim, respectively.

Attias was either oblivious to or didn't care how Hana felt. In the weeks and months it would take Attias to sell his and Ephraim's share of the heroin, Attias recruited Hana for another drug run. This time he wanted Hana to fly two kilograms of cocaine to his brother Itzhak in Bat Yam, a coastal Israeli city south of Tel Aviv.

Itzhak wasn't as criminally minded as his brother, but Attias assured him it was easy money and that the plan would go off without a hitch. By talking to Ron Gonen and Ephraim, Attias knew he could pay $30,000 or $32,000 for the two kilos in New York and make at least twice that much money by selling the drugs in Israel.

But when Itzhak called to say Hana had only delivered one kilo, Attias' profit margin was erased, and he went into a rage. He later found out that Hana had gone ahead and sold the missing kilo himself, keeping all of the profits. Attias was further enraged when Itzhak called to say he had been arrested with the kilo, suspecting Hana had set his brother up.

WHY WOULD JOHNNY Attias, who had killed Alyian Moussan for no discernible reason and at least half a dozen other men on impulse, not kill Elio Hana? Hana had blatantly stolen a kilo of cocaine from Attias and may have had a hand in his brother's arrest. Hana should have been dead the second he returned to New York. Attias' decision to spare Hana's life would ultimately lead to his downfall.

There are a few possible reasons why Hana was spared. The most obvious is that, in addition to being Attias' courier of choice, Hana was laundering huge sums of money for him. Hana had set up Swiss bank accounts in Ofra's name and would periodically wire sums as large as $200,000 to Attias through Ofra. Attias worried he wouldn't be able to tap into the millions of dollars he had in the account if he killed the one man who completely understood how the complex financial web worked.

Attias was probably aware at this point of the power struggle within the Israeli Mafia between himself and Eitan Haya. Killing Hana—who was generally liked— may have swung favour in Haya's direction. Attias had heard that Hana had complained to Haya after Attias had insulted Hana's son. It was clear Haya was trying to use Hana as leverage in his growing rift with Attias. A third reason was simple economics: Hana owed him money for the stolen kilo, and Attias could not get that money if Hana was dead.

While they were barely on speaking terms, Attias consulted with Haya on what to do about Elio Hana. Haya agreed that Hana should pay Attias for the kilo, and even conceded he should pay the full retail value of what it could have been sold for in Israel and not what Attias had paid for it in New York. Attias knew there was no way of proving Hana had anything to do with his brother's arrest, and the lost kilo—as well as most of Itzhak's remaining years—would have to be scrapped as a cost of doing business.

Attias walked to his kitchen and grabbed a list that was hanging on his refrigerator. He wrote down Hana's name and the amount he and Haya had agreed upon. Attias kept the list, there in the open, of everyone who owed him money. His thinking, Ofra would later say, was that if anything ever happened to him she'd know who to track down for money to live off of and raise their three daughters. The list may have prompted Haya, who had followed Attias into the kitchen, to ask about Attias' loan sharking business. The men began arguing.

Haya accused Attias of trying to push him out of the loan sharking business, a business Haya had started working when Attias was still in a French jail cell. Haya was also upset with Attias for protecting Israel Alice (at some point in October 1989, Haya and Israel Alice had a fall out over drugs and money, according to an FBI memo). He told Attias he didn't like the way he had 'slapped' Hana, presumably meaning he felt Attias was disrespecting Hana while overlooking Israel Alice's flaws.

The conversation, which had started with the two men joking, ended with Haya telling Attias he would kill him.

12

HOW TO GET ARRESTED

THE MURDERS AND heroin deals in 1989 temporarily took Johnny Attias' attention away from Ron Gonen, but by August, Ran Ephraim was again putting pressure on Gonen to start dealing heroin for the Israeli Mafia. Beyond that, Ephraim had a ludicrous request: He wanted Gonen to secure 200 kilos of cocaine, which he and Attias were going to sell in New York.

Finding 200 kilos of cocaine was tough even in good times, and 1989 was not a good time to be a midlevel cocaine dealer. Two busts in early 1989—one in Los Angeles involving 1,500 kilos and one in Queens involving 2,000 kilos—had dried up the national cocaine market. Almost overnight the wholesale price of a kilo shot up by $4,000 in New York. Costs for end users doubled and, in some parts of the country, tripled or quadrupled.

Even getting a single kilo for Ephraim was proving to be tough. None of Gonen's usual suppliers wanted to deal with Ephraim, who was developing a reputation as a cheat.

Eliot Danon was still angry that Ephraim had not paid him the commission for the Christmas time deal in late 1988. Rosita and Ephraim had gotten into a spat when she sold him seven fake kilos in April of 1989. It was retaliation for Ephraim shorting her on an earlier deal. Ephraim threatened to kidnap and kill Rosita's teenage son. Only at the last possible moment was Gonen able to broker a truce between the two, avoiding bloodshed.

By May 1989 Gonen determined that Rosita—and not Jaime—had stolen the 20 kilos of cocaine from herself. Accused of stealing the kilos, Jaime had been held and beaten by the Colombians for several days before escaping and hiding, first at Gonen's apartment and later outside of New York City. In May, Rosita left New York just as suddenly as she appeared. Gonen heard rumours that she was returning to the city on occasion and living in Miami, but he never saw her again.

Jaime returned to New York in the summer of 1989 after learning that Rosita had left. He took his usual position in the back room of Mezzanotte, the Italian restaurant Danon operated at 203 First Avenue in Manhattan. Jaime resumed doing odd jobs for Danon and brokering multikilo cocaine deals for Gonen.

At the time, Gonen was selling kilos to a group of Canadians through Michael Weatherby, as well as a man who would travel to Manhattan while on work release from an upstate penitentiary. Keeping them supplied in quantities of six, ten, and 13 kilos was possible with Jaime's help, but even Jaime rolled his eyes when Gonen told him about the 200 kilo deal Ephraim wanted Gonen to broker.

Gonen wanted in on the massive deal, which stood to be the largest in the Israeli Mafia's short history. It would have a six-figure payout and give him a financial cushion to distance himself from the drug business. So Gonen pursued the deal, trying to find a supplier who could help him fill Ephraim's order.

Gonen should have known Hamilton Campos' conveniently timed offer to supply two hundred kilos was a classic case of something being too good to be true. But greed tends to cloud judgment.

HAD HE BEEN born in any other country, Hamilton Campos could have been an international soccer star. But Campos was born in Brazil, the perennial soccer powerhouse and, as a result, was only a slightly above-average player. Campos played semi-professional soccer in his 20s, moved to New York to try to make a team in a fledgling, professional soccer league in America, and—failing to do so—fell into a life of cocaine addiction and crime.

Gonen met Campos in 1986. They were introduced by a mutual friend who knew Gonen had connections in the jewellery business. Campos was looking to sell 1,000 carats of emeralds he had smuggled into the country from Colombia. Colombia sparked a careful conversation about drugs, and before long Campos was telling Gonen he had a friend who was looking to buy cocaine by the kilo.

Billy Lutz was a plumber and a drug dealer, and every seven to ten days he would meet Gonen at

Campos' Union City, New Jersey, apartment and buy a kilo or two from Gonen. Gonen often used these deals to sell the kilos he was buying back from Ephraim.

In the spring of 1989, Campos suddenly disappeared, leaving a cryptic message that he had gone on vacation to Brazil. Gonen continued to sell to Lutz, meeting him in different locations throughout New York and New Jersey.

Campos called Gonen a few weeks after the Markowitz, murder and said he had returned from Brazil. He told Gonen—using the code words they used when they spoke over the phone—that while he was in Brazil he had met a cocaine grower who had 50 kilos he was looking to sell in America. Campos wanted to know if Gonen would help move the product.

'So what the fuck is wrong with you? Are you sick?' Gonen demanded when he met Campos early the next morning.

Campos looked confused.

'You come from Brazil,' Gonen said. 'Where is the suntan?'

Campos brushed off the comment, saying it had been a short trip and the weather had been bad. He wanted to talk business. Gonen was hesitant, even then, but he was feeling pressure to get a good chunk of cocaine for Ephraim, so he listened to what Campos had to say.

The meeting marked the start of the DEA's four-month pursuit of Ron Gonen.

'Here was a guy who used to do a half kilo, maybe a kilo, a week, and now he was saying he had 200 kilos? Something wasn't right. You just don't graduate that quick,' Gonen said. 'But then again, I thought, he had been in Brazil, and there was so much activity in Brazil, maybe he had gotten a connection.'

In reality, Campos had never gone to Brazil. During the six weeks he had disappeared he had been in jail, working out a plea agreement with members of the Group 63 Task Force. Headed by the DEA, the task force was made up of federal and local law enforcement officials in New York and New Jersey and was investigating cocaine trafficking. Gonen was right—Campos was only dealing a half kilo or kilo a week, and that made him a small fish. When he offered a bigger fish, a dealer who was moving multiple kilos every day and dealing drugs internationally, the Task Force was more than happy to cut a deal.

The mere mention of his name was enough to get Gonen's phones tapped, and between 1 July and 19 July, 1989, the DEA listened to Gonen broker six cocaine deals with Jaime. Campos helped them break the code Gonen and Jaime used to discuss the amount and price of the product, but they were not able to use those conversations to catch Gonen in the act. He had, after all, been doing this long enough to keep his cocaine well hidden and the specifics of his transactions—the meeting places and times—off of the phone lines.

Whatever hesitation Gonen had about dealing with Campos quickly disappeared as Ephraim took to dealing cocaine at a furious pace. In August, he arrived at Gonen's Manhattan apartment with five kilos of cocaine, which he cut with Inositol. He arrived the next day with more Inositol and thirteen new kilos of cocaine. As Gonen nervously watched Ephraim work in his apartment, Michael Weatherby called to say he was coming to New York and needed ten kilos.

Weatherby wanted to buy ten kilos for $142,000. Ephraim told Gonen to tell him the price was $17,000 each—'Take it or leave it.'

A few minutes later, Campos called to say he had twenty kilos. Though Gonen didn't hesitate to say he'd meet Campos and another man to work out the details of the deal, he suspected he was in trouble. Even Honey Tesman was nervous. When Gonen was heading to meet Campos and his new supplier, Tesman said she didn't like the sound of the new guy and she had never trusted Campos. She begged him not to go, but Gonen told her they had no choice—they needed the money.

As it turned out, their suspicions were accurate. The stranger was an undercover DEA agent and had Gonen made a deal, he would have been arrested that very day.

Gonen said he needed to think about the deal and would get back in touch with Campos. The stranger warned him he had other buyers willing to purchase the cocaine, but Gonen was firm. He sadly retreated to Danon's restaurant, which had just closed for the night. Gonen sat at a table with Jaime and Danon and accepted the drink they poured him.

'I think I just got busted,' Gonen said.

Jaime told him not to worry—they had, after all, 'just been talking.' But Gonen wasn't so sure. Suspecting he would need the money for his legal fees, he called Ephraim to see if he could bring down his price, after which he called Weatherby to see if he could come up in price. His $500 commission on 10 kilos would not add up to much, but it would be something, and it would be a deal done with people he knew he could trust.

For the group 63 Task Force, the trail on Ron Gonen dried up after that. He stopped taking calls from Campos, and he started using pay phones for more and more of his communication. They tailed him but never did catch him in the act of selling cocaine.

And it didn't really matter. Gonen had implicated himself way back in July when he was less careful and openly spoke about drugs deals with Jaime, Ephraim, and Campos on his tapped telephone line. It was just a matter of getting a grand jury to indict him and finding the perfect time and place to arrest him. The DEA agents and John Guslavage, an Elizabeth, New Jersey, police officer assigned to the task force, consulted with the US attorney's office and shared their evidence. The US attorney said Gonen could easily be charged with six counts of conspiracy to distribute cocaine.

Each count carried a sentence of ten years to life in prison. One of the reasons they did not hear Gonen discuss drugs in the month between his last meeting with Campos and the day he was scheduled to be arrested was that Gonen was desperately trying to get out of drug dealing altogether. He went ahead with the Weatherby deal, but even that turned out to be a bust when Ephraim backed out of the agreement, saying he only wanted to sell six kilos instead of ten at the previously agreed price.

Gonen wrongly assumed he hadn't been arrested because he never carried the drugs in those months when he started to suspect he was being tailed by law enforcement. 'I never checked a law book—I didn't know about conspiracy,' he said.

Honey Tesman started noticing helicopters flying over the Long Beach home. She recalls going into the backyard, tucking her freebase pipe into her boot, and shielding her eyes from the sun to look up at the helicopters. Sometimes they would hover over her for a few minutes and then fly away; on other days, they would stay fixed over the home for hours at a time.

Throughout the late summer of 1989, Gonen was frantic. For years he had put off getting out of drugs, and now he felt he had just weeks, or even days, to put together a plan. He didn't always make wise decisions. Gonen flew Doris Calle to New York; he wanted to introduce her to jewellers to help him in a stolen jewellery scheme he was devising for his life after drugs. At the same time, he started flying Tesman to Berlin to sell kilos of cocaine that he had purchased in New York for $15,000. Frantz—his old safe cracking partner from his days in Munich—was running a brothel in Berlin and said he could pay as much as $60,000 for each kilo Gonen could send.

'I used to fly wherever anybody asked me to fly, because a trip was a trip,' Tesman said of her career as a drug courier. 'It didn't bother me—I was stoned the whole way, everywhere I went.'

She was almost arrested in Berlin on one of these trips. She had flown from New York with Alex Medlos, the Russian lounge singer to whom Gonen occasionally sold cocaine. Tesman called him Tub-A-Lub. Medlos became visibly nervous as Tesman's antics escalated throughout the flight. Tesman, again posing as a pregnant woman, was carrying three kilos in her phoney belly; Medlos, who had been carrying a kilo himself, slipped his product into her handbag. By the time they were shepherded through customs in Berlin, he was drenched with sweat. They were asked to go into an office, where Medlos denied knowing Tesman.

Tesman was oblivious to how much trouble she was in. She flirted with one of the customs agents who questioned her. She told him she needed an inhaler from her handbag, and it would have been impossible for the young, blonde officer to not notice nearly two pounds of cocaine, wrapped tightly in plastic, sitting in her bag.

And yet he didn't say anything. He told his partner that her bag was clean. And then he offered to drive Tesman to her hotel.

THERE IS A photo of Gonen taken in September 1989. He is seated next to Doris Calle in his Manhattan apartment. Both are smiling. Outside of a few more helicopter sightings over the Long Beach home, Gonen had started to figure his law enforcement problems were over. Calle had arrived in New York and was shoplifting the mornings away at a furious pace. In the afternoons, they would take in the typical tourist sites in New York. Sometimes Tesman and Mariel would join them. Other times they'd all convene in Long Beach for long, drunken dinners.

Gonen's ease wouldn't last long.

On the morning of 24 September 1989, Gonen took a cab to his apartment. Before the cab driver could find a place to pull over, Gonen noticed a man on a corner wearing an earpiece. He saw another man across the street, standing at a bus stop, reading a newspaper and wearing a similar earpiece. Gonen knew there were at least two kilos of cocaine in his apartment, tucked into a ceramic cookie jar in the kitchen. He knew he needed to get that and any other drug paraphernalia out of the apartment, but he also knew he would be arrested as soon as he tried to enter. Meanwhile, Calle was spending the day in the apartment, but Gonen didn't dare call her, knowing the phones were tapped.

For the next two days Gonen tried to go home. He spent a small fortune having taxi drivers circle the blocks around his apartment, but it seemed as if every corner was occupied by an agent or someone who might have been an agent. Business ground to a halt—he made only one deal during those days, selling 30 pounds of marijuana to Weatherby. Weatherby owed Gonen $17,000 for the pot and some cocaine he had bought previously and said he'd be back on 28 September to pay him. Gonen resumed his stakeout of the stakeout of his apartment. He took the bus up and down through his neighbourhood. On the third day, he didn't notice anyone wearing earpieces. On the fourth day, he wrestled up enough courage to try to enter his apartment.

Gonen drove his own car back to the neighbourhood. He double-parked in front of a corner store across the street from his apartment and went in to buy a grapefruit and a carton of milk. He wasn't particularly hungry. Gonen wanted his hands occupied so he would appear unthreatening. If he was about to be arrested, he didn't want anyone thinking he was fishing for a gun in his pocket. He didn't want anyone to get jumpy and accidentally shoot him.

He took five steps from the store toward his car and was tapped on the shoulder by Sergeant John Guslavage of the Elizabeth, New Jersey, police department. Gonen looked up and saw six men in various modes of dress surrounding him. No one had drawn a weapon. The men identified themselves as immigration agents, and Gonen was momentarily relieved—his problem, he thought, had nothing to do with drugs. An agent took his car keys and moved his car. The other five herded him into the back of a waiting unmarked car. He was searched—the agents missed a knife and a small bag of cocaine, which Gonen was able to dispose of in the backseat of the cruiser, thereby avoiding additional charges.

The agents led Gonen to his apartment. Gonen told Calle—in English—to open the door. Calle was confused; they always spoke to each other in German. But Gonen didn't want the agents thinking he was telling her to hide anything or, worse, to find a weapon. When she finally opened the door, his apartment was searched, and Calle's documents were checked. Remarkably, none of the five agents searching his apartment came across the kilos in the kitchen. The agents found his shoulder holster but no pistol. Gonen told Calle (who, not being charged with anything, was free to go) to go immediately to Long Beach. She was not to tell Tesman anything but to simply await instructions.

Gonen realised his problems were bigger than immigration charges when he saw the only item the agents had decided to remove from his apartment: Billy Lutz's business card.

Everyone, Gonen remembers, was calm; by the time they led him downstairs to the waiting car, the agents were almost friendly. Before the car pulled away from the curb, Guslavage explained that he was being arrested on drug charges in New Jersey. He could go through the extradition process and spend a few days in a New York jail, waiting for a hearing. Or he could waive his extradition rights and go straight to Newark for his interrogation.

'Take me to Jersey,' Gonen said.

GONEN HAD WATCHED enough television to know he shouldn't say anything until he had a lawyer, so he told Tesman to find him the best criminal defence lawyer she could. Tesman tucked a bottle of wine and a cocaine pipe into a backpack, left Calle to watch Mariel and headed to Newark, where she met with Robert Platz. By that afternoon, she and the attorney were in a federal building in Newark waiting to see her husband.

Before he was arrested, Gonen's world was a world of constant contact. He was the first person he knew who had a portable telephone, and he routinely rang up monthly bills of $2,000 or more. He had multiple pagers: one for his clients, one for his suppliers, and one for his friends. He had another pager for his best clients, and another just for Tesman. He knew which pay phones offered the most privacy in every corner of Manhattan, and he spoke with his accomplices several times a day. His biggest concern at that moment was getting out, even if only for a few hours. If he didn't answer Ran Ephraim's pages within minutes, if Eliot Danon couldn't track him down or if Jaime stopped by his apartment and didn't find him there, people would begin to ask questions.

And those questions would lead to speculation that would stumble on the truth: Gonen had been arrested, and if he wasn't killed, he might turn on his friends.

When the lawyer first arrived, Gonen had it tucked in the back of his mind that he could be bailed out and then immediately jump his bail. But even if they allowed him to post bail—a huge improbability given that he was a classic flight risk—where would he go? He could get his hands on $7,000 at the Long Beach home and collect the money Michael Weatherby owed him. Establishing the bankroll to leave drugs and New York behind had been hard enough without the watchful eye of law enforcement tracking his every move. Getting away with just over $30,000 would be impossible.

There were other factors. Although his cancer had been in remission for over a year, Gonen needed to constantly check in with a doctor to make sure he was healthy. And if the cancer came back, he wanted access to top-notch medical care—something he felt he wouldn't be able to afford in hiding.

But the biggest motivation was his family. Gonen knew they'd be lost if he became a fugitive. Tesman was and always had been a mess. Sitting in his cell, it wasn't long before Gonen was able to picture her holding Mariel and standing on a welfare line. Since Gonen had quit drugs five years earlier, he had offered some stability to Tesman's otherwise chaotic world. His wife would be dead or destitute and his daughter lost to foster care if he fled.

The lawyer spoke matter-of-factly. The task force had built a strong case against Gonen, and even if he went to trial, his odds of winning were almost nonexistent.

'If you plead not guilty, I'll need $250,000, and you'll still have a good chance of losing,' Platz said. 'Or you can plead not guilty, and pay me $50,000. You're still taking your chances, but they're better chances, and they're cheaper chances.'

It was also clear to Gonen that if he could co-operate and testify against his friends, he might win favour with the court for a reduced sentence. Going to jail seemed inevitable—minimising the time he spent in jail was his only chance for minimising the destruction Tesman could inflict on their daughter.

As it turned out, Tesman had already started inflicting damage on the agents who had arrested her husband. She was drunk and undoubtedly high, and as she waited to see her husband she screamed and spit at anyone who came near her. Her husband was a victim of entrapment, Tesman said, and she and Gonen were going to fight it. Tesman would maintain this position for years, hating the fact that her husband was forced into being a rat.

Even as Tesman screamed about their willingness to fight the charges in the tile-lined corridors of the federal building in Newark, her husband was preparing to do what had once been unthinkable. Working with Guslavage, Gonen began outlining the details of his dealings. It became a give-and-take game of truth or dare. Gonen would offer up some information, and if it checked out, Guslavage would help him in ways most inmates wouldn't be assisted. Gonen was able to place calls to the people who would be most suspicious of his absence and explain he was in Canada and wouldn't be available to meet.

But during this time, there were no signs that Gonen was going to be freed. And with each passing day, he grew more and more frantic. The Jewish holiday Rosh Hashanah was approaching, and for the past several years, Gonen had celebrated it with the Ephraims. The longest stretch he had gone without seeing Ephraim since they had both returned to New York was seven days, and if Gonen wasn't there for the holiday, Ephraim would be beyond suspicious.

And, given the company Ephraim now kept, his suspicions could be deadly.

JOHN GUSLAVAGE WAS slowly starting to trust Gonen, and the more he dug into the case, the more he realised it could be the kind of case that makes a law enforcement career. It touched on a brutal gang of thugs—foreigners who had flaunted US laws and, in the process, had left an untold number of people dead or drug addicted.

There were two main issues facing his informant. Gonen needed to collect the $17,000 Michael Weatherby owed him—no drug dealer would leave that sum of money on the table or even hold off on collecting it. And Gonen needed to be seen by Ran Ephraim to assure him everything was normal. Guslavage conferred with federal prosecutors who had started looking into the Israeli Mafia in New York after Raz Ben-Zvi paid for a $20,000 addition to his home all in $10 bills. Ben-Zvi, who had been so worried about going to prison after the $8 million gold robbery, had gone ahead and done something that all but made it a self-fulfilling prophecy. The investigators on Long Island explained that Ephraim was a rising player in a deadly gang, and even if he couldn't bring himself to kill Gonen, plenty of his accomplices would gladly do it.

Beyond that, Gonen could gain far more information and evidence on the street and by talking to Ephraim in the comfort of his own home than he could in clipped telephone calls from the federal building.

Guslavage, whom Gonen had already started calling Gus, agreed to let Gonen out for the holiday as a trial run. He wanted to see if Gonen could be trusted and what kind of evidence he could get.

They allowed Gonen to drive his own car home, the same 1985 Oldsmobile he had double-parked in Manhattan when he was arrested a week earlier. But he certainly wasn't alone. They drove in a convoy, complete with an assortment of unmarked agency cars, from Newark to Long Beach, allowing Gonen to arrive home a few hours before Ephraim, his wife Judith, and his stepdaughter were scheduled to arrive.

Tesman was irate that the task force agents were in her home and told them as much as they tried to prep her husband. As they affixed bugs to Gonen, they prepped him on things he could say to get information out of Ephraim. Gonen went over his story of where he had been for the past week, but, most important, he tried to convince Tesman that they needed to play along if they expected to live through their current crisis.

Tesman reluctantly agreed. The evening was uneventful, and, perhaps because he was already suspicious of Gonen, Ephraim barely spoke about business. He did mention that he and some of their other friends—most notably, Eitan Haya—were growing frustrated with Johnny Attias. They felt the gang was spiralling out of control and that Attias was cutting everyone, except for Israel Mizrachi, out of their scams. It was interesting listening for the agents monitoring the wire taps and for Guslavage, who was hidden in a closet off the dining room. But it wasn't nearly enough to build a case against Ephraim or any of the men he mentioned.

The biggest boon of the night was an added dose of trust for Gonen. Guslavage allowed him to make arrangements to collect his money from Michael Weatherby. When the collection went off without a hitch—with Guslavage hiding in the closet of Gonen's apartment—the cop began trusting his prime informant. That trust would be crucial for bringing down the Israeli Mafia—and keeping Ron Gonen alive long enough to testify.

13

AGENT RON

ONCE GUSLAVAGE KNEW Gonen could be trusted, Gonen was allowed to leave the cell in the federal building serving as his home each day and work the streets as he normally would. He would return 'home' each night, handing back the specially designed Cross pen and lighter he had been given, complete with a tiny microphone for recording conversations.

The Task 63 Task Force wanted Eliot Danon and Jaime, believing they were the link to a larger Colombian drug cartel that pumped hundreds of kilos of cocaine into New York each month. They knew it would be easy to build cases against Weatherby, the Canadians, and a string of other midlevel dealers who came to New York to buy cocaine from Gonen.

And most of all, they wanted Ran Ephraim. They believed they could flip Ephraim against members of the Israeli Mafia. After that, the Task Force would work with the U.S. attorney's offices in Newark and the Eastern District of New York to build cases against the Israeli Mafia, and Gonen would enter the federal

Witness Protection Programme with his family—after he served an as yet to be determined jail sentence.

Gonen made dozens of phone calls and set up countless meetings. He bought and sold drugs, all under the watchful eyes and ears of Guslavage and the Task Force. But what they could have never guessed from the recordings was that there was a bigger problem looming.

The Israeli Mafia—now being openly speculated as the group behind Michael Markowitz's still unsolved murder—was on the verge of civil war.

Gonen needed to be arrested—again.

Gonen didn't like the idea of spending each night in the converted cell in the Task Force's office at the federal building in New Jersey. And his concern wasn't limited to personal comfort. Tesman reported that Ran Ephraim had begun asking questions. He wanted to know why he never saw her husband at the Long Beach house anymore and why Gonen never picked up the phone at his Manhattan apartment. If Gonen was officially and publicly arrested, he could make bail and perhaps have a convenient excuse as to why he was having trouble filling Ephraim's ever-increasing orders for kilos of cocaine.

It was a risky move. There was no way to predict how Ephraim would react. Gonen assumed that Ephraim would pressure him to jump bail and flee with Attias' help, but if Ephraim felt threatened, he might kill Gonen.

Guslavage formulated a plan. When Gonen met with Michael Weatherby two weeks earlier, he had hinted it wouldn't be long before he had a cheap shipment of cocaine to sell. The key was to arrest Gonen and Weatherby so it would appear as if Gonen had no prior knowledge of the bust. Gonen called Weatherby to tell him the cocaine had arrived and that he could bring his broker to meet Weatherby later that night. The broker was an Italian-American DEA agent.

They met in a deserted parking lot just off a highway in Fort Lee, New Jersey. Weatherby was accompanied by two of Gonen's Canadian customers, Sean and Michael Gould. They were in town visiting Weatherby, and when they heard Gonen had cheap kilos to sell, they asked to come along. Gonen got out of the car and hugged Weatherby—they had not seen each other in two weeks. For a moment, Gonen hesitated, knowing he was about to ruin this man's life.

They moved into Gonen's car and Gonen introduced his broker. Guslavage monitored everything with other agents from a nearby electronic surveillance van. When the deal was completed and Weatherby and the Goulds got out of the car, chaos ensued.

Seemingly out of nowhere a half-dozen cars tore into the parking lot and surrounded the two cars, which were parked head to head. Four men jumped out of each car. All were wearing bullet-proof vests and had guns drawn. Weatherby and the Goulds were ordered to lie facedown on the ground. Gonen and the DEA agent played along and followed orders to get out of the car slowly, with their hands up.

Each man was loaded into a separate car. Guslavage was in the front seat of the van Gonen was put into; the two men did not speak until they were clear of the parking lot. Gonen watched Weatherby being placed into handcuffs and then into the backseat of a different car. Gonen would never see Weatherby again.

As the car carrying Gonen pulled away, Guslavage told him he had done a good job. He would be booked and processed, and his arrest would become public. He would have bail set, and, like all prisoners, he would get one phone call.

Gonen called Ran Ephraim.

Ephraim didn't say much, other than ordering Gonen to call him as soon as he raised bail and was released. As it turned out, it would take Gonen ten days to raise the $100,000 bail, and that only happened when Tesman convinced a family friend to put her house up as collateral.

Ephraim wanted to meet in Long Beach, preferably at his apartment. If not there, they should meet at Gonen's house, Ephraim said. Guslavage was sitting across a table from Gonen as he talked on the telephone with Ephraim and shook his head 'no.' Both he and Gonen knew it would be easier to kill Gonen in a private residence. Gonen suggested Eliot Danon's restaurant. Ephraim reluctantly agreed.

Danon smiled when Gonen entered and the two men hugged. 'Poppa,' Gonen said, 'it's been a bad month.'

Danon was not happy to see Ephraim. He was still upset over the non-payment in the cocaine deals earlier that year. Ephraim grunted a greeting at him and then told Danon to leave them alone. It was midafternoon. No customers were in the restaurant and Ephraim led

Gonen to a secluded table in the back of the room. As Gonen went to sit down, Ephraim stopped him and patted him down for a listening device.

For Ephraim, it was an exercise in futility. The Task Force had access to the latest equipment and had outfitted Gonen with a specially made pen and cigarette lighter, each of which hid a tiny microphone. Gonen simply pulled out his cigarettes, lit one, and placed the box and his lighter on the table between them. The entire conversation was now being recorded.

Ephraim did not talk about himself or his dealings. He wanted all of the details of Gonen's arrest and what had happened in the ten days since. Ephraim was mainly trying to figure out what Gonen had told the authorities about their dealings and what he planned to do.

'I'm going to plead guilty,' Gonen said.

Ephraim was dumbfounded. Getting caught and going to jail was not something either man had ever contemplated. The plan had always been to flee back to Israel once you made bail. Gonen said it was a chance he could not take. He was too worried about what would happen to Tesman and Mariel.

'Did you talk about us? Me? Johnny?' Ephraim said.

'No,' Gonen said. 'It's not a betrayal. I just need to plead guilty and do my time. It's the only hope I have for a light sentence.'

Ephraim told Gonen he didn't need to go to jail. Ephraim had spent several months putting together a shipment of 500 kilos of cocaine that he wanted to move in Europe. Ephraim had finally found a Colombian willing to fill the entire order. Earlier that month Ephraim, Johnny Attias, and Israel Mizrachi had flown to Los Angeles and found a boat captain who agreed to transport the cocaine to London. Gonen could board the boat when it stopped in New York, jump his bail, handle the deals in London, and live the rest of his years as a wealthy man in Europe.

For a split second the proposition tempted Gonen, but all he had to do was look at the gold-plated cigarette lighter sitting on the table to know he would never be able to take part in the deal. And even if he did, getting on a boat controlled by Ephraim may have been a walk to his own funeral.

Gonen told Ephraim he'd think about the offer. That meant Ephraim would be calling Gonen several times a day for the next few weeks, asking him if he had made up his mind. And as Gonen continued to stall, Ephraim would grow increasingly frustrated and increasingly suspicious. He could have—and, perhaps for his own sake, he should have—killed Gonen. But because of his association with the Israeli Mafia, Ephraim had other problems.

After the meeting concluded, Gonen sealed Guslavage's trust for a final time. Despite agents waiting outside of the restaurant and peppering the corners surrounding Messanotte, the Task Force temporarily lost Ron Gonen. He was seen leaving the restaurant and hugging Ephraim before they parted ways, but he was quickly swept up in the midday Manhattan crowds.

For Guslavage, the next 30 seconds seemed like 30 years. Gonen had been swept up in the lunchtime crowd, and now none of the agents radioing in to Guslavage could locate him. Finally an agent who had frantically left his post to begin hunting for Gonen was tapped on the shoulder . . . by Gonen. Gonen had no idea, but by reasons completely unintentional, he had been a fugitive for half a minute.

Guslavage relaxed. Ron Gonen could be trusted, and, with his help, Guslavage had the chance to bring down one of the country's biggest narcotic import/ export operations.

A 4 NOVEMBER 1989, investigator's report notes that sometime in the previous month, Eitan Haya and Israel 'Alice' Mizrachi—by then Johnny Attias' most trusted confidant—had had a falling out over 'drugs and money.'

Joe Reich was starting to complain that Attias was bleeding the gas tax skimming business, taking a bigger cut than Markowitz had demanded while doing none of the work the Russian had put into keeping the scam in order.

Elio Hana was still stinging from his demotion to common drug courier. And Haya was just plain tired of Attias. That had been a month earlier, when Haya didn't know where the rest of the Israeli Mafia stood on Attias' leadership. Now it seemed as if he had almost enough backing to assassinate Attias and take control of the gang.

The last key was Ephraim. Only Ephraim and Israel Alice could get close enough to Attias to plot his moves and figure out the best time and place to commission the hit. Israel Alice would be loyal to

Attias until the end, but Haya knew Ephraim had shifty morals. He knew Ephraim had originally hitched on to Attias because Ephraim saw him as the alpha male, the leader who would dole out rewards for loyalty. If Ephraim saw that power base weakening, he could be convinced to back an emerging leader. Haya began slowly politicking with Ephraim, trying to figure out how deep his loyalties to Attias ran.

By Hanukkah, the answer would be not very deep at all.

Attias was having a holiday party. For a while it seemed as if the quibbling within the Israeli Mafia had been put on hold, if only for an evening. Their wives drank and ate upstairs, while the men drank in the finished basement. Ephraim had contemplated inviting Ron Gonen to the party but thought better of it. Ephraim knew Attias might kill Gonen if Gonen showed up. Attias was frustrated that Gonen had first refused an offer to deal heroin and was now refusing an offer to baby sit 500 kilos of cocaine on their way to London. He speculated that Gonen was a rat, and Ephraim couldn't offer credible evidence to counter the claim. Gonen had been acting strange since his September trip to Canada and his October arrest, and even Ephraim was beginning to have suspicions about him.

Indeed, since the fake arrest, Ephraim and other members of the Israeli Mafia had been trying to test Gonen's loyalties. Every time Ephraim offered another reason why the London trip was a perfect plan, Gonen threw up another excuse.

At first, Gonen protested by saying he was still wanted in London for the fraud ring, but Ephraim knew the seven-year-old charges were barely being pursued, and, as a master document forger, Gonen could create identities in the time it took most people to cook dinner. When Ephraim challenged him on that excuse, Gonen retreated to his defence that he worried Mariel wouldn't be cared for and his cancer would not be treated properly if he fled.

'What about Honey?' Gonen had said.

'I can take care of her, if you want,' Ephraim said.

'Take care of her?' Gonen said. 'How?'

'I don't know. With a gun,' Ephraim said. 'Or we could make it look like an accident.'

Gonen didn't want Tesman dead. He wanted her provided for. Tesman was the mother of his daughter, and, even after all of the problems she had caused him, Gonen loved her.

What Gonen never told Ephraim was that he believed that if he got on that boat, he would be killed as soon as he got to London, if not before. He would be dumped at sea and forgotten, leaving behind a widow and a helpless, four-year-old daughter.

If Ephraim's suspicions were correct—that Gonen had done more than get himself arrested, that he had agreed to co-operate—it would be difficult to kill him in New York. Not impossible, as the Italian Mafia had proven on dozens of occasions, but it would be risky. And he wanted to be certain Gonen was an informant. They had, after all, been friends for almost 20 years. Before he confirmed the Gonen problem with Attias,

Haya, or other members of the Israeli Mafia, he needed to be certain Gonen was a rat.

As Gonen continued to refuse the offer, the phone at his Long Beach home started ringing at odd hours. Someone was playing head games with Gonen. Whoever was behind the calls was trying to raise a reaction out of him and see how he dealt with being called a rat. Sometimes the caller would say nothing. Other times the caller would make cryptic comments. One night, when Gonen was staying in Manhattan and Tesman was home with Mariel, two men started banging on the door. Tesman had never seen the men before. She opened the chained door a crack to ask what they wanted.

'Tell Roman we know,' one man said before both turned away.

They had used Gonen's birth name, the name he had dropped two decades earlier while living in Israel. Only his closest friends and family members still called him Roman. Whoever was behind the head games knew Ron 'Roman' Gonen well.

No, Gonen wasn't at Attias' Hanukkah party in early December 1989 because Ephraim still wasn't certain if Gonen was a friend in trouble or a foe making trouble. But Johnny Attias was at the party, playing cards and drinking hard at a table in Ephraim's basement.

There are differing accounts of what happened next, but almost everyone who was in the basement would say that Attias—as he was prone to do—got drunk and drew his gun. It was a small gun, fashioned to look like a cigarette lighter, but it was still a gun. These moments were normally filled with nervous laughter as Attias was capable of killing for no reason even when he was sober.

What is clear is that at some point during his tantrum, Judith Ephraim came down the basement stairs to see if the men needed anything. Attias pointed the gun at her and fired. The bullet whizzed past her head, burying itself in the wood panelling of Ephraim's finished basement. Ephraim probably didn't confront Attias, who was still holding the gun, but he was angry that his wife had nearly been killed. The party broke up, and, presumably, not long after that night, Haya told Ephraim about his plan to get rid of Attias.

BUT IN THE end, it may have been Ron Gonen who signed Johnny Attias' death warrant. If Ephraim had any reservations about killing Attias, an off hand comment made by Gonen may have pushed his decision.

Gonen was planning a much-needed vacation. He was spending his days at the federal building in Newark, helping agents decode the hours upon hours of recorded conversations he had been compiling. He was such a fixture at the federal building that members of the Task Force started calling him Agent Ron, and much to their pleasure, Gonen was collecting solid information. By night, Gonen went on with his drug dealing, setting up coke buys that would add to the pile of evidence the Task Force was collecting on the biggest drug traffickers in the tristate area.

His work didn't end when, tired and weary, he made it back to Long Beach. Gonen was trying to convince Tesman about their next move. Their next move meant fleeing the life they had grown accustomed to in

New York and starting over in the Witness Protection Programme.

Tesman had aggressive confrontations with Guslavage. 'You're just the other side of the coin,' she told him. 'You're doing the same thing as us, you just figured out how to do it legally.'

Even though she knew every phone conversation was being tape recorded, Tesman tried to drop hints to Ran Ephraim every time he called.

'I was trying to tell him to get out of town,' she said later. 'I didn't want to see anyone get busted. Everyone at the DEA hated me.'

Hoping to help Gonen make his argument that they needed to enter the Witness Protection Programme, Guslavage played tapes on Ran Ephraim offering to shoot Tesman for Gonen. They played her tapes of Ephraim telling Haya he would kill Gonen, Mariel, Tesman, and Tesman's older daughter if he found out Gonen was a rat. And yet Tesman still dropped hints.

'I didn't believe them,' Tesman said. 'I knew Ran loved me. He said he loved me because I had balls bigger than any man he knew.'

It was a stressful period in their marriage. The only time Tesman spoke to her husband without contempt for his decision to rat was when Gonen told her the agents had missed the cookie jar full of cocaine in his Manhattan apartment when they had executed their search. Tesman drove to Manhattan and did not return to Long Beach until she had put a huge dent in the two kilos Gonen had hidden there.

Gonen was developing an ulcer and needed to get away. Perhaps as a preview of what their new life would be like, he packed the family up for a ten-day trip to Hershey, Pennsylvania. It was close enough that Gonen could still make it to Newark or New York if he was needed, but far away enough that he wouldn't bump into anyone he knew. While the city is noted for its amusement park in the summer, the dead of January wouldn't offer them much in the way of entertainment outside of a tour of a chocolate factory, a barren Pennsylvania landscape, and a motel television set.

Gonen met with Ephraim to let him know he wouldn't be available for a while. He said Tesman had relapsed and he needed to get away. Ephraim mentioned that Johnny Attias had been arrested. He had been pulled over for a broken tail light, and when the police officer searched the car, he found a hand gun.

But Attias had been released after just five days. 'That's strange,' Gonen said.

'What's strange?'

'Well, they would have fingerprinted him, and they would have seen that he wasn't who his phoney documents said he was,' Gonen said. 'I thought he would have been deported, not released.'

'I was fingerprinted first thing,' Gonen said. 'And they would never let him go without establishing his identity.'

'Do you think he's a rat?' Ephraim said.

'No ... I don't know,' Gonen said. 'Probably not. It just seems strange.'

A few days later word filtered back to New York about a major drug bust in Amsterdam. Several kilos of cocaine that had been earmarked for New York had been seized, and Attias' Dutch supplier, as well as the courier charged with delivering the drugs, had been arrested and were looking at hefty prison sentences. The timing seemed too coincidental for Ephraim, who was out tens of thousands of dollars on the deal.

'You were right,' Ephraim said the next time he spoke with Gonen. 'That motherfucker ratted us out.'

14

DANNY FISH

JOHNNY ATTIAS HAD been at the Sea Dolphin for most of the night on 18 January 1990. He had been having dinner and drinking with Israel Alice and two other men. Attias cautiously flirted with the women—his wife Ofra had said she would stop by the Sea Dolphin restaurant later that evening.

The gangsters loved the Sea Dolphin. It was a Kosher Italian restaurant with a nautical theme, run by Daniel Joshen. The gangsters took to calling it 'Danny Fish.' It was in Queens, in a hard scrabble neighbourhood. The food was good and cheap, and Joshen was a little too timid to speak up when the gangsters didn't tip the servers or, even worse, walked out on their tabs. Best of all it was the type of place where they could talk about business openly. They knew everyone who would think of eating at Danny Fish, and any outsider who did venture in wouldn't feel welcome.

Just after 10pm, Attias looked at his pager and saw that Ran Ephraim was calling him. They had been playing phone tag all day; Attias needed to speak with

Ephraim, and Ephraim, apparently, needed to speak with Attias. At 10.26pm Attias excused himself from the table and called Ephraim from the pay phone at the front of the restaurant.

Ephraim asked where Attias was eating dinner and noted that he could hear Israel Alice in the background. Attias quickly changed the subject—Elio Hana was late in paying Attias $5,000, and he wanted to know if Ephraim had talked with Hana. Hana owed Attias $250,000 and the $5,000 was supposed to be a partial, good faith payment. He wanted to know if Hana was planning on stiffing him.

'You know I'll hit him,' Attias told Ephraim. 'You know I'm really nervous about him.'

Attias was nervous about a lot of things that night. It remains unclear if he was indeed the informant who set the Amsterdam heroin bust in motion, but it is clear that the men within his crew held that belief. And three hours earlier he had heard from his friend David Azouly, who said Eitan Haya had been shaking him down for money. The holiday spirit that had resulted in a temporary truce between Haya and Attias had dissipated and Attias had called Haya about his threats to Azouly.

'If you don't leave David alone, I'll fuck you in the ass,' Attias said. 'I'd make sure you don't leave the house.'

Attias said he had things to discuss with Ephraim. Before hanging up they made a plan to meet the following morning at 10am at Attias' house.

Ephraim had no intention of going to the meeting.

THEY HAD BEEN planning this night for weeks. At 10.34pm, just after he hung up with Attias, Ephraim paged Hana. Hana called back a minute later, and Ephraim told him that Attias was eating at the Sea Dolphin. Israel Alice was there, and Ofra would be there later. It sounded as if Attias was on the verge of being drunk. It could be their best and last chance to execute their plan before Attias sobered up and made good on his threats to Haya.

Hana hung up and made another call. At 10.38pm he called Ephraim back to say he had met with his friend. The friend would never be identified, but it was later learned that Eitan Haya had given that friend a photograph of Attias and $50,000 earlier that week.

Ofra Attias arrived at the Sea Dolphin at 11.30pm and wiggled into a booth next to her husband. He had just finished his dinner and was laughing over drinks with Israel Alice and his other dinner companions. A few minutes after his wife arrived, Attias excused himself, saying he needed to get something from his car, which was parked in front of the restaurant.

Attias had $8,055 in cash tucked into his pockets. The trunk of his 1986 Oldsmobile was strewn with trash, so it is unclear what he was retrieving from the trunk when he left the restaurant. There was a bag of Mannite, a common cutting agent for heroin, on the backseat of the car. Attias opened the trunk and bent over the back of the car, fishing for something in the darkened well.

His friends in the restaurant later reported hearing three or four gun shots, followed by Attias screaming, 'They shot me in the ass!' A car had slowly rounded the corner as Attias had bent over the trunk of the car, and a gunman had fired at least three shots from the open passenger's widow. Attias had been hit twice in the buttocks and the car sped off down the deserted street. The first bullet came out of his upper right thigh, while the second cut upward, hitting several internal organs before exiting through his upper right abdomen.

At first the wounds seemed more embarrassing than deadly, but Attias was losing a good amount of blood. He was in pain and asked Ofra to take him to the hospital. Ofra was hysterical, so Joshen and Addula Asouri—a regular at Danny Fish who knew Attias in passing—loaded him into a car for the ride to Kings County Hospital.

Until her own death in 1999, Ofra would claim doctors at the hospital had botched her husband's treatment. The doctors hadn't acted quickly enough and hadn't seen how serious his gunshot wounds were.

Johnny Attias was pronounced dead at 1.10am on 19 January 1990.

AT 3.44AM RAN Ephraim called Eitan Haya. He had just received word that Attias had died.

'It is reason to wake you up, sweetheart,' Ephraim said to Haya. The two men talked excitedly for nine minutes and made plans to meet at Haya's house early the next morning. But by the end of the conversation they were both so worked up that their plan had succeeded that Haya told Ephraim to come over right away.

Judith Ephraim stopped by Haya's house early the next morning. Haya had still not showered, and her husband was happily sipping coffee and smoking cigarettes in Haya's living room. Despite not having slept, Haya and Ephraim were talking at an excited clip. They were both visibly happy.

'You see?' Haya said to Judith as she entered the room. 'I did it.'

In the end, it had been Ephraim, Elio Hana, Haya, and Haya's wife Leora who had put together the plan and raised the money to get rid of Attias. Judith asked Leora how the shooter had known who Johnny Attias was. Leora said they had given the shooter a photograph of Attias and a description of his car.

Haya wasted no time in taking over the day-to-day operations of the Israeli Mafia. He knew Israel Mizrachi would collect for Attias to support the widowed Ofra, so he began compiling a list of everyone who owed Attias money. Topping the list was Elio Hana and Mickey Salter, a produce importer who was friendly with members of the Israeli Mafia.

'There aren't anymore big shots in this world. Every dog has his day,' Haya told Salter when they met to discuss his debt. 'I give you a pardon. You don't have to pay anymore.'

Joe Reich also called. The one thing Attias had provided him was protection in the gasoline business. Everyone knew that Israel Mizrachi would suspect someone within the Israeli Mafia a had killed Attias, and Reich—who had openly complained about Attias— seemed like a likely candidate for commissioning the hit. The irony was that Reich had not known Attias was going to be killed. Haya promised he'd be given a new bodyguard.

Haya made it clear that no one would be safe until they had killed Israel Alice. He called Salter back.

'Borrow from Israel Alice as much as you can,' Haya said, 'because he will go, too.'

Ofra Attias was emerging as another potential problem. Ephraim had been put in charge of deflecting suspicion from his and Haya's role in her husband's murder. But with Attias' death, Ofra stood to lose between $250,000 and $300,000, despite Israel Alice's best efforts to collect for her. Even Ephraim told Ofra if she accepted anything less than $200,000 from Reich as a buyout for her husband's role in the business that she 'was a sucker.' Reich further angered Ofra by dropping her and her daughters from the gasoline company's health insurance programme, a perk that was worth about $400 a month. When Ofra confronted him about the lapse in coverage, Reich claimed it was an oversight.

Much as he had after Markowitz had been killed, Reich made a pass at the widow. Unlike Markowitz's wife, however, Ofra didn't reciprocate. Ofra wanted more than sex and health insurance—she wanted money. And she had enough knowledge of everything from the Markowitz hit to the four-kilo heroin deal to wield some leverage.

'If Joe Reich won't help,' Ofra said during the Shiva, 'I'll open my mouth.'

It was up to Ephraim to keep Ofra in order and, if necessary, kill her to keep her quiet. He was supposed to console the widow and make sure she was taken care of, all while deflecting suspicion from the true perpetrators of the hit on her husband. But doing so became impossible, because on 30 January 1990, Ran Ephraim was arrested.

THE MORNING AFTER Johnny Attias was fatally shot, a pager chirped in a drab motel room in Hershey, Pennsylvania. The Gonens had spent an uneventful week in Hershey. Tesman seemed relieved to be away from the lies she was forced to tell in New York, but being out there was taking its toll on Gonen.

There is a photo of Gonen taken in the motel room. It is a stark contrast to the photo taken of him and Doris Calle just days before he was arrested. In that photo, Gonen is smiling and happy. In the motel room, he is lying facedown on a bed, his chin crooked in his hand and his elbow resting on the mattress. Four-year-old Mariel is lying on his back and looks at the camera. He dangles a cigarette over the edge of the bed with his other hand. Gonen's expression is sad and pensive.

He was a man living in uncertainty. While he seemed to be keeping his government handlers happy, Gonen had no idea when he would be sentenced and for how long. And just before they left for Hershey, Ephraim had questioned him on whether he was cooperating with the government.

'If you cooperate, the streets will kill you,' Ephraim told him before hanging up.

Ephraim had suspected him as far back as October. On 12 October, Gonen spent most of the day trying to get Ephraim to meet a person who was looking to sell several kilos of cocaine. He called Ephraim's house three times, and each time he was rudely rebuffed by Ephraim's wife Judith. Finally, during the last conversation, Judith told him that Ephraim believed Gonen was an informant.

'If Ran wants to go to prison, he can do that alone,' Judith said before hanging up.

But Ephraim had never made a move to kill Gonen. Their friendship was nearly two decades old, and they had helped make one another rich. Ephraim would not kill Gonen until he was absolutely certain that Gonen was co-operating.

And now, with Ephraim's number popping up on Gonen's pager, it seemed as if he was certain.

'You need to get back to New York,' Ephraim said. 'We need to meet. Johnny has been killed.'

Ephraim offered only the vaguest details of the shooting but did made a thinly veiled comment implying that Gonen was lucky it hadn't been him. Ephraim had urgently needed to meet with Gonen several times in the months since he had been arrested, and Gonen had survived all of those meetings. But there was something different in Ephraim's tone this time. It was part sadness, part anger, and part remorse.

Gonen packed up his family and headed back to New York. He never told Tesman why they were cutting their vacation short on the long drive back to New York, but he believed he had, at best, a 50% chance of surviving his next meeting with Ephraim.

DEA agents monitoring phone lines in New York, however, would never let Gonen attend that meeting. Later that same afternoon they overheard Eitan Haya call Eliot Danon and tell him to not talk to Gonen.

'He's a rat,' Haya said. Danon, who had loved Gonen like a brother, was stunned.

Gonen stopped in Newark to check in with the agents at the federal building before driving back to Long Beach. He went in expecting instructions on how to handle Ephraim. But instead of being instructed on what to say during the meeting, Gonen was told to get his family ready to disappear. The time to move Ron Gonen, Mariel, Tesman, and Tesman's daughter into the Witness Protection Programme was now.

30 JANUARY 1990, was a long day for members of the Group 63 Task Force.

Gonen, his wife, daughter, and stepdaughter had been escorted safely to the Long Beach home. Gonen rounded up ten high school boys, friends of his stepdaughter, to help load a moving van. Given that Ran Ephraim lived in an apartment a half a block away, it was a risky move. For four days agents had been using a silver Mercedes to tail Ran Ephraim, but they needed to time his arrest to the perfect moment. If they arrested him too soon, his associates might be able to get to Gonen before he could be safely whisked into anonymity; if they waited too long, Ephraim might notice Gonen was gone and attempt to flee.

Armed US marshals manned each end of Gonen's block. His stepdaughter's friends nervously eyed the men wearing black nylon jackets and brandishing shotguns as they packed the moving van with furniture and boxes. None of them realised it would be the last time they would see their friend's father and mother.

Tesman was reluctantly going along with the move. She had repeatedly threatened to stay behind, but there were problems with that set up. Even if Tesman's life wasn't in danger—and wire taps proved that she was definitely being targeted—Gonen was not a naturalized US citizen. Without a wife, Gonen would be unable to work when they got to wherever it was they were going. He would face deportation back to Israel where associates of Attias, Haya, and Ephraim could get to him. And in the end, she realised that more than anything else, she still loved Ron Gonen.

'I couldn't bear the thought of keeping Mariel from him,' Tesman said. 'It would have killed him.'

When the Long Beach home was loaded up, they made one last stop at Gonen's Manhattan apartment. Once again the street was closed off, and armed marshals watched as Gonen moved a few possessions from the apartment into the moving van. By the time they were ready to pull out, the Tuesday afternoon rush hour was starting. On a good day, it takes just under three hours to drive from Manhattan to the Gonens' first destination in anonymity, Lancaster, Pennsylvania. With the traffic and the circuitous, indirect route the convoy took in case they were being followed, the trip took twice as long.

But even with Gonen and his family safely handed off to the US marshals, which oversee the Witness Protection Programme, the Group 63 Task Force's work in Long Beach was not done. Just before midnight on 30 January, a team of DEA agents kicked down the door of Ephraim's Long Beach apartment to execute a search warrant. All three people—including

Judith's 13-year-old daughter—were handcuffed. At his arraignment the following day, Ephraim's lawyer would complain that a loaded gun had been held to the teenager's head during the arrest.

By all outward appearances, it appeared as if the Ephraims had been getting ready to run. There were boxes packed and stacked near the entrance of the apartment, and artwork had been taken down and left leaning against the walls of the living room. The furniture was under dust covers.

While they knew Ephraim had played a massive role in the execution of Johnny Attias, they did not yet have enough evidence to charge him. Besides, they were hoping to lean on Ephraim to build cases against the two remaining players in the Israeli Mafia—Eitan Haya and Israel 'Alice' Mizrachi. The two men had hated each other before Attias was murdered and now they were on the verge of launching a full-scale gang war against one another.

What they did have on Ran Ephraim were four counts of conspiracy to distribute cocaine, courtesy of Ron Gonen's co-operation. Each count, for deals ranging from one to six kilos, carried a sentence of ten years to life. Judith was being charged with conspiracy as well, stemming from a June 1988 drive she took with Gonen and her husband to sell two kilos in Elizabeth, New Jersey. When the penalties for the charges she was facing were added up, Judith faced up to 40 years in prison and $2 million in fines. Judith was particularly culpable because while her husband was very careful when he discussed business with Gonen over the telephone, Judith openly talked about 'merchandise' and large sums of money.

Ran and Judith Ephraim pleaded not guilty to the charges they were facing on 1 February. The couple listed monthly bills totalling $2,000 and disclosed that they had $100,000 in a Las Vegas checking account. They also owned two properties in Las Vegas valued at a total of $140,000.

Eitan Haya and Elio Hana quickly began working to raise Ran Ephraim's bail. They approached everyone they knew hoping they could convince someone to put their house up as collateral. But everyone they knew also knew how Attias had intended the system to work: bail would be raised, and the accused criminal would flee to Israel. Everyone assumed that Haya was hoping to keep the same bail-and-flee policy in place.

A wiretap on 8 February showed that Haya had emerged as the new head of the organisation. And as late as 13 February he was warning people that Ron Gonen was an informant, unaware that Gonen had been hiding in Lancaster for two full weeks as he waited to be processed into the Witness Protection Programme.

Haya would end up regretting his decision to help Ephraim.

At some point between the 1 February arraignment and 8 June 1990, investigators convinced Ephraim that he was going to jail for a long time. They showed him how easy it had been for them to translate the Hebrew he had spoken to Haya in the hours after Johnny Attias had been murdered. The conspiracy to commit murder charge—a capital crime—made the four cocaine charges seem relatively minor.

On 5 June, Ran Ephraim agreed to change his plea on the drug charges to guilty. Those charges would eventually be dropped when he later agreed to plead guilty to conspiracy to commit murder charges. By doing so he avoided a life sentence without parole. Three days later Judith Ephraim changed her plea as well and was released on $250,000 bail. At a bench conference during her change of plea hearing, lawyers confided to the judge that Judith and her husband had agreed to become co-operating witnesses and were expected to enter the Witness Protection Programme. Like Ron Gonen before him, Ran Ephraim had betrayed his friends to protect himself.

And the end result was chaos for the Israeli Mafia.

WHEN HE ARRANGED to have Johnny Attias killed, Eitan Haya made himself the head of an unravelling organisation. By August the Israeli Mafia was in such disarray that Haya resorted to making an attempt on Israel Alice's life himself.

There had been bad blood between the two men for nearly a year. Haya wasn't pleased that Mizrachi had gone ahead and tried to collect debts owed to Attias on Ofra's behalf after Haya himself had forgiven the debts. Fortunately for Mizrachi, Haya was a better gunman than a bomb builder.

Mizrachi's nephew, Moshe Cohen, was visiting from Israel and staying with the Mizrachis that summer. On 12 August, Mizrachi loaned the teenager his gold 1987 Lincoln. On his way back to Mizrachi's Brooklyn home that night, he stopped at Hamir Peset, an Israeli social club, for a drink.

Cohen hadn't been in there long when people came running into the club, yelling that a gold Lincoln was on fire. Witnesses reported seeing a man running away from the car. Because of his dark complexion, Haya was described as 'Puerto Rican or black' in police reports. He dumped a badly burned jacket and a charred New York Mets baseball cap before running from the scene.

When he was arrested in connection with the death of Johnny Attias and other charges more than a month later, investigators noted the burns on Haya's arms. At first Haya said he had injured himself while fixing his own car, but he later confessed that even a month after he had tried to kill Mizrachi with a poorly constructed car bomb, the burns had not healed.

EITAN HAYA WASN'T the only member of the Israeli Mafia to be arrested on 17 September 1990.

Using information from Ron Gonen and Ran Ephraim, investigators were able to get indictments against eleven members of the Israeli Mafia, including Haya, Elio Hana, Israel 'Alice' Mizrachi, Josi 'Joe' Reich, and Ofra Attias. They would make nine arrests that day. Hana and Mizrachi fled the country before the arrest warrant could be executed. Hana was eventually captured in Bolivia and returned to the United States, where he became a co-operating witness in the trials and plea negotiations against the other ten.

Eliot Danon—the unassuming Israeli restaurant owner—was also arrested. An arrest warrant was issued for Jaime, Danon's trusted confidant, but he remains at large. After receiving the tip from Gonen about the $4 million gold robbery, investigators were able to use testimony from Ephraim to build cases against Raz and Luiz Ben-Zvi. Ephraim eventually served six years in prison and lived for a time in the Witness Protection Programme. He is now believed to be living in hiding and near poverty in the Middle East.

In addition to Gonen, Ephraim, and Hana, Ofra Attias agreed to co-operate. After her husband's murder, Ofra had worked with Yoav Sinah to gain control of the heroin trade Johnny Attias had built up. After her arrest, Ofra Attias tried to maintain her innocence.

'If we didn't have the tapes, I would have believed her,' said Eric Seidel, then an assistant district attorney with the Brooklyn DA's office. 'She was an attractive woman and came in crying with these big blue eyes.'

But it didn't take long to convince her she was in trouble. By 1 February 1991, Ofra Attias had changed her plea to guilty and, like Gonen and Ephraim, had been whisked into the federal Witness Protection Programme. She was 35. After serving her prison sentence, she lived in Texas under an assumed identity before returning to Israel. In 1999, while on vacation in Spain, she was killed in a car accident.

Even Israel 'Alice' Mizrachi and Joe Reich couldn't outrun their American crime spree. Both had returned to Israel: Mizrachi when the indictments were handed down and Reich when he was able to jump bail. Both men had returned assuming they would be protected by an Israeli law that prohibited the extradition of

Israeli nationals to face trial on capital crimes in a foreign country.

But in 1993—after significant pressure from US authorities—an Israeli judge ruled that Mizrachi and Reich could be tried in Israel for their role in the Markowitz murder, even though the murder had been committed in the United States. It was an unprecedented and difficult way to try a case. Seidel, who speaks Hebrew, made countless trips to Jerusalem to help Israeli prosecutors prepare and argue their case. Gonen and Ephraim testified via closed circuit television from a Manhattan courtroom, and, because Mizrachi had told her he was the shooter, Ofra Attias became a star witness and was flown back to Israel to give her testimony.

Also testifying was a top Luchese family turncoat, Anthony 'Gaspipe' Casso. Mizrachi and Reich were eventually acquitted of the murder charge after a trial described as 'something out of Damon Runyon.' But largely because of Ofra's testimony, Mizrachi was convicted of smuggling four kilos of heroin from Amsterdam to New York and sentenced to 12 years.

Eitan Haya was dealt with harshly by the US justice system, partly because he refused to give up the name of the person he hired to kill Attias. He spent 16 years in a US prison before being released and deported to Israel in late 2003. There he was reunited with his son Aaron, now 23 and a rising star in the Israeli underworld.

RON GONEN'S WORK as 'Agent Ron' for the Group 63 Task Force didn't end with his help in collaborating with investigators working on the Israeli Mafia cases. In addition to providing information that allowed cases to be built against Attias' henchmen, Gonen brought down a string of drug dealers operating in the northeastern United States.

Ron Gonen continued to work with the government until 1995. He gave testimony and was flown from his secret location in the Witness Protection Programme to meet with prosecutors who were either preparing cases against his former associates or, more often than not, seeking information to use as leverage in their attempts to get people to plead guilty.

Michael Weatherby was convicted and sentenced to ten and a half years in prison. He also forfeited his home and vehicles. Co-defendants in the case, including the Gould brothers from Canada, received sentences between six and 20 years.

Billy Lutz was sentenced to six years because of Gonen and eventually agreed to co-operate. His co-operation led to the conviction of a Newark, New Jersey, councilwoman on a corruption allegation.

Perhaps no one would end up cursing Ron Gonen more than Eliot Danon. Danon was convinced that accepting commissions and allowing Gonen to use his restaurant to broker cocaine deals was not nearly as bad as some of the crimes Gonen and his associates had committed. Told he was facing dozens of years in prison even if he did plead guilty, Danon chose to fight the charges.

Over four days in October 1991, Ron Gonen testified against Eliot Danon, the man who had given him refuge when he was battling cancer and needed a break from his wife. Gonen spoke bluntly about their dealings. Defence attorneys worked hard to portray Gonen as an untrustworthy criminal looking for a break in his own pending sentencing, but Gonen swayed the jury. Tape-recorded conversations showed that Danon was more than a small business owner who couldn't say no to his unscrupulous friends. Through Jaime, he was a direct link to a Colombian cocaine cartel.

Despite poor health and a failing heart that caused his 1991 trial to be temporarily suspended, Danon was sentenced to 16½ years in prison.

Someone eventually caught up with Israel Mizrachi.

Mizrachi served his time and boldly moved back to Tel Aviv after his release from an Israeli prison in 2001. The underworld in the city was largely controlled by a rising star in the world of gangsters named Aaron Haya—the then 20-year-old son of Mizrachi's former nemesis, Eitan Haya. Eitan Haya was still in America, serving out the remainder of his 16-year prison sentence on the conspiracy to commit murder charges.

Mizrachi lived a law-abiding life in the high-security Diesendorf Towers near Herzl Street, Tel Aviv's main commercial drag. He bought into the Carmel Market and opened a chain of food stands and bakeries called The Brothers Mizrachi. His neighbours considered him a millionaire 'with an interesting past,' according to one Israeli newspaper account of his life.

On 6 August 2003, a bomb went off on Herzel Street, destroying a silver Mercedes sport utility vehicle. Initially investigators thought it was another act of terrorism in a city all too accustomed to bomb blasts. But when they saw the precision with which the bomb exploded and how efficiently it killed the lone occupant of the car without doing damage to nearby buildings or injuring bystanders, they started to suspect otherwise.

'It was so professional that a nearby gas station wasn't damaged,' a police spokesman said. 'Only a highly skilled professional is capable of such a hit, and in Israel, we don't have too many professionals who could do this.'

Police got their confirmation that the explosion was a gangland hit a few hours later when they identified the body in the SUV as that of 58-year-old Israel Mizrachi.

No one was ever charged in the murder, but there has been open speculation about who was behind the hit—even if he was still in a US prison.

Eitan Haya was deported to Israel a few months after Israel Mizrachi was murdered. He had served 16 years in a US prison and had not been in Israel for more than 20 years, but he quickly regained his position atop the Tel Aviv underworld with the help of his son Aaron.

Haya is also the only member of the Israeli Mafia who is believed to still be operating as a criminal. He lives in a highrise apartment known as City Gates in the Ramatgan section of Tel Aviv and drives a BMW sport utility vehicle. He operates with 24-hour bodyguard protection.

15

HIDDEN

When I should have been playing with Barbies, and thinking boys had cooties, I was in a federal relocation centre. When I should have been spending holidays with my family, I was on a plane flying across the country, being put in a situation where I would never know what it was like to have aunts and uncles, cousins, nieces, nephews, grandparents, or a sibling. I was put in this situation because no one had ever taught my father that crime never pays until it was too late.

—Excerpt from a December 1999 letter from Mariel Gonen to a US District Court judge asking for leniency in the sentencing of her father on drug distribution charges.

Ron Gonen drives a Lexus. It's nearly 15 years old and breaks down every few weeks, but when his friends at the upscale bar where he likes to hang out ask him what kind of car he drives, he can say a Lexus.

But on this day late in the summer of 2005, Gonen is going to sell the Lexus. He's hoping to get enough money to repair his daughter's car. Mariel is 20 and heading to college, and Gonen doesn't want to take any chances that she'll break down between home and her destination. But before he can dump the car at the lot where he used to work as a used car salesman, before Gonen can give the mechanic the go-ahead to make the repairs, they need to track down Mariel's medical records. Universities are stingy when it comes to childhood immunisations.

For most parents, such a task is as simple as calling the family practitioner's office. But for Gonen, it involves trips to three different doctors before he finds one who will write a letter noting Mariel is in good health without mentioning he was unable to review her childhood immunisation records. He also makes a trip to her elementary school to track down copies of her health forms. Combined, the incomplete documents will hopefully be enough to convince college health officials that his daughter won't come down with a case of polio.

'Daddy, why is my life so messed up?' Mariel says as they climb into the Lexus after a second doctor has turned them down. If kids rebel against their straight-laced parents by getting into trouble, Mariel has rebelled by being a do-gooder. She spent two years volunteering for various nonprofits after high school graduation and now she's off to a small college back east.

Gonen is proud that his daughter is getting the education that he never did. He's also proud that she got arrested last year.

'Just like her father,' Gonen beams.

But the difference is clear: Mariel got arrested during a political rally. Gonen got arrested for being a gangster. Gonen became a co-operating witness and now he, Mariel, and Gonen's estranged wife are all trying to live happily ever after in the federal Witness Protection Programme.

Gonen starts the car and then juggles a cell phone and a hand-rolled cigarette as he eases into traffic. He dials the US marshals' office, his guardians since 1990, hoping they'll be able to offer a solution to his medical record dilemma. He hasn't had too much contact with the marshals since 1995, when he finished giving testimony as a government witness in cases against 12 of his former accomplices, but he can always call in an emergency. He's hoping this will qualify as an emergency.

Gonen mumbles their dilemma into the phone— he needs childhood immunisation records for Mariel, but all those records are under their pre-programme names. Gonen hangs up by the time they are pulling into the parking lot of the third doctor's office.

'What did they say?' Mariel asks.

'They said, "Sorry, nothing we can do,"' Gonen said.

IT TOOK SEVEN months to find them a permanent home. If Gonen didn't have drug-dealing contacts in a given city, then Tesman had family there. They were initially relocated to St Paul, Minnesota. But at the last minute Tesman's daughter decided she didn't want to join her mother, stepfather, and half-sister in the Witness Protection Programme. The girl—who was 16 at the time—already knew her family's new names and where they were moving to and so officials had to start the process of finding the Gonens a new home. It was also gut-wrenching for Tesman, who would no longer be able to see her daughter on a regular basis.

For Gonen, now 58, the city they ended up in was a culture shock. After having spent most of his life in some of the world's most famous cities, nothing had prepared him for the sprawl-free outposts of flyover country.

'On the first day we drove five or six miles. I see some tall buildings over there and that was it—everything else is flat,' he said. 'To me, it didn't look like a city at all.'

Things didn't look up when Gonen navigated the city bus system to go downtown. He was hoping to find work and buy a car with the $3,500 stipend offered by the government. He found a used car lot in a bad part of town, and, before he even had a driver's license in his new name, he had a job selling cars. 'Selling cars, selling coke. What's the difference?'

Junkies dealt in a nearby park and burned-out buildings were on either side of the small garage. At night, two vicious looking dogs patrolled the 20 or so cars that served as the dealer's inventory. Gonen resolved to hold the job for only as long as it would take to get the realtor's license that had eluded him in New York. If that didn't work, the government had offered to put him through nursing school.

'If this city looks like this, this is going to be difficult,' Gonen said at the time.

But then on his way home that evening, he found a glimmer of hope—a small jazz club. Gonen believes a city has something going for it if it has a good jazz club. It's the same jazz club he frequents to this very day.

GONEN HAS HANGOUTS. He takes his morning coffee at Starbucks, and on weekends he goes to a Borders bookstore to read the international newspapers. There's the jazz club. There's a neighbourhood bar with every conceivable import beer for sale where Gonen can buy the same beers he drank when he was a master safe cracker in Europe in the 1970s. There's a fern bar that caters to the upper-middle-class 50-somethings that Gonen pretends to be, and a hip bar a few blocks over where Gonen seems to fit in, even though he's a generation older than most of the other patrons.

The owners and bartenders in each place greet Gonen with a smile, and waitresses and hostesses offer him hugs. When he has cash—after closing a real estate deal or a good weekend in Vegas—Gonen tips well and buys drinks for everyone he knows. He hasn't had cash for some time—it's February and his last closing was in September—but they're still happy to see him. Everybody likes Gonen, but few people in his new life really know him.

Most nights end at the jazz club, where a five-piece ensemble is playing in the spacious but crowded backroom and the bar is doing a steady Saturday night business. The bartender asks how his mother has been doing—she's 85 and has been sick. Then a waitress wiggles up next to Gonen at the bar. She is barely 30. She takes the black beret from his head and puts it on her own, then rubs a hand over Gonen's closely shaved scalp. It is clear that she likes him, and for the past several months Gonen has had an on-and-off relationship with her.

'I get off at one tonight, but I may get out early,' she says hopefully.

'Not tonight,' Gonen tells her.

It's not that Gonen doesn't like the girl. And women seem to adore Gonen. But when they get too close, they start talking about marriage and a life together. And that means Gonen either has to break it off or let them in on the truth. Gonen has been separated from Tesman since 1994, but he cannot get a divorce. If they get a divorce, Tesman will leave the programme, and if Tesman leaves the programme, Gonen gets kicked out. He loses the papers that allow him to work legally in the United States, and he could be deported to Israel, where some of the people he testified against went after they finished serving their jail sentences. As a result he tries to keep Tesman as happy as possible, and that includes supporting her financially on his meagre, on-again, off-again income.

When he first arrived here, Gonen told people he was an art and jewel dealer who had been a defendant in a tax evasion case that had ruined him financially. Coupled with the one true part of his story—that his wife was a cocaine addict—Gonen said he moved to a new city where they didn't know anyone for a fresh start. When women wanted to get more serious, he would tell him he wanted Mariel to have a stable life without a string of girlfriends moving in and out of her home. On two occasions, he liked the women enough to tell them that he was in the Witness Protection Programme, and, lucky for him, those two women were good at keeping secrets.

But Mariel grew up and moved away, and the men he hangs out with in the different bars have picked up on the fact that most of Gonen's personal history seems to begin in August 1990, when he moved here.

I had expected someone living in the Witness Protection Programme to be a bit more inconspicuous, but when I meet his friends from the fern bar, he introduces me as 'the writer who is writing about my life.' I make a joke about being a writer from *Real Estate Digest.* They chuckle, but when Gonen isn't listening they press me for details.

'So he was a spy, right? He was Israeli intelligence,' one of them asks.

'I think there's more to that tax case. He did time, didn't he?'

There's a lawyer at the bar, and he knows more about Gonen than any of the other men. He helped Gonen prepare his case when it finally came up for sentencing in 2000. After referring most of the work to attorneys in New Jersey, Gonen was sentenced to time served—just 42 days—and fined $50. Gonen's lawyer sees I'm getting increasingly uncomfortable with the direction the conversation is taking.

'Maybe we're better off not knowing,' the lawyer says. The other men laugh, thinking the lawyer is joking, and return to their drinks. Later, at the jazz club, it's clear that the waitress knows even less about Gonen's past than the men he has been drinking with for years.

'Are you sure?' the waitress asks. 'We could just get a drink somewhere.'

'Not tonight,' he says again. Gonen doesn't know if he likes this girl enough to tell her the truth.

She puts the beret back on Gonen's head. She pouts, turns away and mutters, 'I need to check on my tables.'

THE MEN OF the Israeli Mafia did not quickly forget Ron Gonen. Gonen testified at Israel 'Alice' Mizrachi's trial in Israel via a closed-circuit television hook-up from Manhattan. After the trial ended in 1995, his mother, who was still living in Tel Aviv, started getting death threats.

In June 1996, a man approached Gonen's mother and told her that her son had harmed his associates. 'They will not forget what your son did, and we will find him and he will pay for it,' the man said.

Gonen's mother was threatened two more times, once in person and once over the telephone. Gonen called the US marshals' office, and they arranged to move his mother from Israel so she could join her son and his family in the safety of the Witness Protection Programme.

Gonen's mother gets a monthly social security cheque. Some months are so tight that Gonen has to take money from the cheque for gas money.

AFTER HE GOT his real estate license and showed his first house—an elegant, $400,000 home in the nicer part of town—Gonen called the US marshals' office and said he needed a psychiatrist.

The client had shown up on a Saturday morning, and Gonen called to get the lockbox combination for the key of the house he wanted show. The house was gorgeous, and today it would easily sell for seven figures. As the potential buyer walked through the kitchen, Gonen noted all the silver in the adjacent dining room. When the buyer checked the master bathroom, Gonen opened the bedroom closet to see how many furs the sellers had. When the buyer paused in the living room, Gonen got on all fours to check the quality of the Persian carpets.

'I have keys to all the houses in town,' he said. 'I could set up a phoney showing, get the combination, make a copy of the key, and come back a week later and steal everything.'

In those first few weeks, Gonen showed that he had a knack for real estate. But when he would close a deal, instead if taking the closing fees straight to the bank, he would keep it for a few days to remember what it was like to walk around with $4,000 in his pocket—'Just to feel like I'm still alive.' Finally the marshals called back with the name of an FBI approved psychiatrist.

When the psychiatrist asked Gonen what he wanted to work on, he told her, 'Teach me how to walk the streets without any money. I feel naked.'

Like 82% of the 17,000 or so government-protected witnesses, Gonen has never been accused of another crime. By comparison, only 60% of the people paroled from prison go on to lead crime-free lives. But to this day, it is a constant struggle, and it took Gonen a long time with the psychiatrist to start to feel like he could make it as a straight man.

GONEN'S ONE LISTENING is scheduled for an open house. For Gonen, the condominium is part investment, part storage unit. It is barely furnished with a few of his belongings, and on the 11th-storey balcony overlooking a downtown skyline, he keeps paintings he has collected, as well as sheets of poster paper with crudely drawn roulette wheels and notes on Gonen's gambling system. The system works, he says, but then quickly concedes he lost $5,000 during his last trip to Las Vegas.

The unit is spotless. Gonen is hoping to find a buyer who will pay $10,000 or $11,000 more for the unit than he paid ten months ago. The unit is, however, quiet, save for the Sinatra he plays from a stereo in the master bedroom. Lately business has been tough, but real estate always appealed to him. When he worked for an agency he knew enough English to fake his way through the reports and his paperwork, but now that he's on his own it comes down to the raw components of capitalism: spotting a good deal and salesmanship.

'Selling is selling,' he says. 'Do you need cocaine or do you need a house? What's the difference?'

But the difference is clear an hour into the open house when the phone hasn't rung and no one has buzzed the doorbell. Cocaine is recession proof, and 15 years ago Gonen could make $60,000 by simply putting his wife on a plane to Berlin with a couple of kilos of blow. Now he's lucky if he makes $60,000 in a year.

'I wish people would come, but maybe no people will come for the whole three hours,' Gonen says.

Still, he's not bitter. Even with no money to buy back his beloved Lexus and no solid prospects, Gonen has everything to be thankful for.

'Where would I be?' he said. 'Dead? Deported? In jail? All three? That's where I would have been.'

POSTSCRIPT
5 JUNE 2007

AT THE OUTSET of my work on *Blood & Volume: Inside New York's Israeli Mafia*, re-titled *Blood and Money* outside the US, I knew there were certain people I would not be able to interview during the course of my research. In some cases it would take days of phone calls and sifting through court records to determine if someone was living or dead, little on figuring out where they were now. It was a frustrating problem but something I was able to work around by extensively interviewing everyone I could make contact with.

There was, however, one figure I desperately wanted to interview and could not: Ran Ephraim, Ron Gonen's best friend and arch-enemy.

A prosecutor who helped convince Ephraim to testify against Eitan Haya and his other cohorts in the Israeli Mafia described him as gregarious and, to a certain extent, likable. He wondered why I would want to write a book about Ron Gonen when, in his opinion, Ran Ephraim was the much more interesting character.

'He was a real pisser,' the prosecutor said. 'He was a funny guy—always good for a story.'

By interviewing people who knew Ephraim I started to develop an idea of what he was like and I hope that not only is that image accurate, but that it carries through in the text of the book. Yet, despite my best efforts, I never was able to locate Ephraim. As the US version of this book went to press in early 2007, my best information said that Ephraim had served his six-year prison sentence in the US, lived for awhile in the US Witness Protection Programme and eventually returned to the Middle East, where he was living in near poverty.

All that information was accurate, in a sense, but it also downplays how dramatic Ran Ephraim's life was after the events chronicled in this book ended.

True, Ephraim did return to the Middle East and, relative to the lavish lifestyle he lived while running with the Israeli Mafia, his finances could be considered near the poverty level. But Ephraim had done more than return to the Middle East—he returned to Tel Aviv, where he openly worked as an art dealer.

And that was Ephraim's downfall. Like Ephraim, Eitan Haya returned to Tel Aviv after serving out his 16-year US prison sentence in the conspiracy to commit murder charges stemming from the assassination of Johnny Attias.

So it was shocking but not surprising when Ron Gonen and I learned that Ran Ephraim had been shot and killed on 1 February 2007 in Tel Aviv. The Israeli press openly speculated that the drive by shooting from a motorcycle had been conducted as retaliation for Ephraim's co-operation with US prosecutors in the early 1990's, and some reporters boldly placed the blame on Eitan Haya. Their speculation was confirmed a few months later, in May, when Haya was arrested after two men claimed they had been hired to kill Ephraim and had also botched a hit on Yoav Sinai, a driver and bodyguard to Johnny Attias. Sinai accompanied Attias on at least two of the murders depicted in this book. Following her husband's murder, Ofra Attias worked with Sinai to retain control of her husband's heroin and loan sharking business—businesses that had been coveted by Haya.

The 2007 attempt on Sinai's life in Israel is perhaps the most tragic: the would-be assassins targeted the wrong man, and a completely innocent father of four was left paralyzed—simply because he had the same name as a former Attias henchman.

'It was a normal morning. We went down to the car on our way to work. We were parked across from our building. I got inside the car with (my wife) Simone. As I was reaching for the safety belt, I saw a man wearing a motorcycle helmet standing a yard away from me, holding a handgun. Before I thought to do anything, he started shooting. He fired two rounds. One slammed into my arm, the other punctured my lung,' the innocent Sinai told the Israeli newspaper Haaretz. 'I saw him coming my way to finish me off. I tried to crouch, I lifted my legs. He shot two more rounds. The bullets hit my legs.'

At the time of writing in June 2007 it is not clear what will happen to Haya in the Israeli court system.

As an American, I was raised in a culture that glorifies gangsters in film, books and television programmes. As a journalist, I was sickened when I thought too hard about these being real stories and real people. Those conflicting sets of feelings would often come together, and I would frequently become infuriated when Ron Gonen showed a lack of remorse for the crimes he committed, or when he laughed at Eliot Danon, who received a massive prison sentence after Gonen co-operated with investigators and walked away nearly Scot free.

'I'm proud of you, baby,' said the woman I was dating at the time of the book's US release. 'But it freaks me out that you know these people.'

And yet when Gonen called one week after Ephraim's murder to say he had been thrown out of the Witness Protection Programme because of his co-operation on the book, I became worried. As infuriating as he could be, I had grown to like him in our two years of almost daily contact. His termination from the programme meant he faced possible deportation to Israel, a virtual death sentence given that Haya and his son are looming figures in Tel Aviv's underworld.

At the time of writing, Ron Gonen continues to live in hiding and is working with immigration attorneys to avoid deportation. The deportation would only apply to Gonen—not to Honey or their daughter, Mariel, who are both US citizens.

This book was written to entertain and to inform readers about a small slice of New York City history. The characters are real people and engaging because they chose to live lives most of us could not begin to fathom. Yet in all of this, I think it is important to remember that before these men were characters, they were violent criminals with real victims, ranging from innocent men like Yoav Sinai and his family to the dozens of men who have been killed in New York and Israel since 1982, not to mention the thousands of people whose lives were ruined by the drugs these men sold throughout the world.

Dave Copeland
Boston, Massachusetts
June 2007

ACKNOWLEDGEMENTS

RON GONEN, HONEY Tesman, and their daughter Mariel opened up their lives to me, and without their help, this book would not have been possible. Ron spent countless hours helping me figure out the correct spellings of names, establish a timeline, track down documents, and piece together the events that largely took place when I was still in high school. More important, he spoke candidly and honestly on subjects and events he was plainly embarrassed about and remorseful of having been a part of, knowing they would be included in this book and expose him to the judgment of readers. Such honesty takes an incredible amount of courage, and, were the roles reversed, I'm certain I would not have been able to do it as gracefully as Ron did.

John Guslavage of the Group 63 Task Force and Eric Seidel, formerly of the Brooklyn district attorney's office, were also crucial in helping to make this book an accurate portrayal of the Israeli Mafia. Guslavage helped me confirm Gonen's depiction of events, and

Seidel, now with the Manhattan district attorney's office, made thousands of documents, photographs, and transcripts available to me.

At Barricade Books, publisher Carole Stewart saw the importance of this story and gave me a chance to tell it when other publishers said no. I am proud to be among the talented, gutsy, and sometimes-controversial authors who call Barricade home. Ivy McFadden provided the much-needed handholding and support that every first-time author craves and frequently amazed me in her ability to help me get my act in order and put this thing together.

Much of the work on *Blood and Money* was conducted as part of my degree requirements in Goucher College's master of fine arts in creative non-fiction writing programme—a truly incredible experience I recommend wholeheartedly to anyone who has a passion for non-fiction writing in its many forms. Pete Earley—a tremendous journalist I hope to model my career after—taught me how to navigate the murky waters of professional publishing. Pete not only helped me frame this story, but also he made it stronger with his thoughtful critiques and his endless list of suggestions on ways to report it. I cannot envision a better mentor or friend.

Also at Goucher College, Patsy Sims, Suzannah Lessard, Philip Gerard, and Tom French—all incredible non-fiction writers in their own right—dedicated their time and wisdom to make me a better writer. All of them had a hand in guiding this project from idea to finished book, and this would not have been possible without their help.

Christine Dellamonaca, college roommates Michael Rodriguez and Frank Mullen, summer camp pal Noah Bullock, and Ilan Greenberg of the *New York Times Magazine* all took on the thankless task of volunteering to read my rough copy as I took this book through a string of drafts. Their thoughts, comments, and input were invaluable.

Outside of the writing process—but still a direct and important part of this project—are my friends and family. Unfortunately space prohibits me from mentioning everyone who offered encouragement and advice, but it would be criminal not to mention the following people:

My biggest regret of the whole process is that my father did not live long enough to see me fulfil my lifelong dream of publishing a book. My Mom and Dad have supported me every step of the way. Growing up, my parents did not pigeonhole my sisters and me into one job or another, but instead gave us the simple instruction to find a career that would make us happy.

Mom and Dad, I'm happy.

My sister Joanne, her husband David, and my nieces—Sara, Emily, and Catherine—opened their home to me on the frequent trips I needed to make to New York and New Jersey to conduct research. They helped me decipher train schedules first thing every morning and made sure a glass of wine or a cup of tea was waiting for me when I returned after a long day of research. Beyond that, they were some of my biggest supporters and believed in this project even when I started to have my own doubts.

Brad Davidson has been my best friend and my biggest promoter for 22 years. On the frequent occasions when I would complain about the string of awful newspaper jobs I had during that time, he would simply suggest, 'You should quit and write a book.' It was simplistic career advice, and for a long time I disregarded it as moronic in its failure to take into account how monumental of a task that can be.

As usual I should have listened to Brad a lot sooner.

Finally good writers need great dogs. Cosmo fits the bill and was the necessary distraction I needed when I had spent far too many hours in front of a computer.

Dave Copeland
Boston, Massachusetts
August 2006